Storytelling With Charts – The Full Story

The Ultimate Playbook to Master the Art and Science of Captivating Audiences by Telling Stories With Data and Framework Charts

BY

SAM SCHREIM

Important

Before Getting Started, Get the Most Out of This Book: Download the Visual Companion Pack

Bring this book to life with downloadable graphs, tables and slides. I've received feedback that the static visuals don't allow you to fully experience the strategies. That's why I'm providing a companion download, containing **83 pages** of high resolution, easy-to-read versions of every chart and diagram.

As an added bonus, you'll also receive a quantitative charts cheat sheet for quick reference when working with data.

With these dynamic digital assets in hand, you'll be able to follow along and visually grasp each concept. See firsthand how mundane datasets transform into captivating revelations that compel audiences. Watch as intricate information becomes unforgettable narratives.

Unlock the full potential within these pages. Visit

www.storytellingwithcharts.com/bookcharts

now to download the complete visual companion set and actively apply what you learn. With crystal clear charts and visuals at your fingertips, abstract ideas will spring to life, propelling your Storytelling with Charts skills.

Claim your visual learner's package now – let's bring this book into full view together!

Table of Contents

Introduction

A poet would be overcome by sleep and hunger before (being able to) describe with words what a painter is able to (depict) in an instant. —Leonardo da Vinci

The most powerful person in the world is the storyteller who set the vision, values and agenda of an entire generation that's to come. —Steve Jobs

Storytelling is arguably the most powerful tool a human being has. As highly social creatures, we use stories to connect with other human beings on emotional and intellectual levels. In doing so we create bonds between ourselves and others. Through storytelling, we create relationships, friendships, families, and even entire communities. Politicians tell stories to their voters about their visions. Brands tell stories to their consumers about who they are. As individuals, we even tell ourselves stories about who we are to motivate, teach and entertain ourselves. According to Yuval Noah Harrari, it was storytelling that gave us human beings the ability to create belief systems, relate history, and even dream of the future (Harari et al., 2018). All this is because there's power in a good story. Think back to your childhood. Odds are there are several stories that you grew up hearing and still remember to this day.

There are in fact multiple kinds of storytelling and visual storytelling is one of them. Dating back to the stone age with their cave paintings, visual storytelling is probably the most impactful form of storytelling. This is because visuals convey a richer experience than text-heavy methods of communication. It's also because they communicate information a lot quicker than paragraphs of writing do. This is one of the main reasons why storytelling with charts—that is to say storytelling using impactful charts–is an incredibly effective way of communicating information. This is especially true in a day and age where the average person visits 89 websites per day and has seven different social media accounts in a quest to get instant information (Roothman, 2018).

This book is all about how to tell a powerful story using storytelling with charts (STC). STC is a very powerful and strategic method of communication that's been around for nearly 60 years. Despite this, few people have been able to truly master it. Having given presentations throughout your academic career and work life, you might think that you are one of those few. The unfortunate truth, however, is that you most likely are not. But you can learn to attain such mastery in due time and with dedication. Attaining this mastery requires understanding which visuals to use and how to use them according to the STC method. Our surveys and studies show that using powerful visuals that meet all STC requirements, like in the below example, increases audience engagement by 80%. It also increases audience retention by 65% and story believability by a whopping 99%!

As an example, consider the two flags in the image below. These flags will, truthfully, look identical when they're hanging on a pole. There are essentially only two differences between them: one of these products is both more expensive than the other and comes with a story.

This is just one example, illustrating how a 50x difference between price points of like-for-like products can be attributed to the story-price premium. Audiences tend to be more engaged in stories than facts and stories are incredibly effective ways of getting them invested in products and ideas. This is why things like content marketing have become major fields of their own. The fact is, stories are powerful because they pack various experiences and beliefs into neat packages and communicate them to both the one telling the story and the audience. During this process, the audience's brainwaves actually synchronize with the teller's (Renken, 2020). This phenomenon is known as neural coupling and it makes it very easy for the teller and audience to communicate shared goals and then actively move toward them. They allow for trust to be formed between storytellers and audience members. These individuals can then start building a productive relationship with that trust.

Another interesting effect of listening to stories is that, getting to the climactic, stressful or dramatic moments of a narrative causes your brain to release cortisol. Cortisol is the hormone that's responsible for your fight-or-flight response. It also plays a part in solidifying memories of emotional experiences and thus having them stored in your brain. Meanwhile getting to the resolution of a story—the part in the narrative where conflicts are resolved, problems are solved and things begin to wind down—causes the brain to release oxytocin. Oxytocin is a hormone that facilitates social bonding, as well as feelings of contentment, calm, and even a sense of security. When you use STC effectively, then, you allow your audience to experience all of this. Your audience forms a more emotional memory of the story they're listening to and thus become more likely to remember it. They form a greater bond with it and associate the narrative that's being relayed to them in the STC with feelings of contentment, calm, and security. Considering all this, it's no wonder that Yuval Noah Harrari has claimed that human civilizations and societies could not have been built if we didn't know how to tell stories (Harari et al., 2018).

The various effects of storytelling are essentially why customers are willing to pay more for the flag that comes with a story. It's also why creating and telling good, effective stories are crucial in the business world. So, how do you go about creating good stories in the business world? A good story within this context needs to accomplish a variety of things. First, it must effectively and accurately communicate the data and information that need to be communicated. Otherwise, why are you even telling this story in the first place? Second, it must provide its audience with some context, meaning that it must relate the given facts to specific kinds of people (i.e. the target audience), places, and events. It must allow the listeners to derive meaning from that which they're listening to.

Who Is This Book For?

Everyone, regardless of what profession or field of work they're in, will need to use and/or write presentations at some point. This includes industry professionals, entrepreneurs, consultants, civil/public servants, academics, students, and more. It includes my wife, for instance, who owns her own business and is preparing a pitch for acquiring VC funding and getting a business loan to launch her startup. It includes my 15-year-old daughter who's campaigning to be the president of the school council and is therefore preparing a presentation sharing her campaign promises with the student body and explaining why they should elect her. It even includes my nephew who has had to prepare one presentation after another for his various college courses and is currently preparing one of his thesis defense presentations.

If that's the case, then who is this book for? The short answer? You. The longer answer? This book is for anyone and everyone who needs, uses, writes, and designs presentations or decks for their line of work. It doesn't matter whether you're using PowerPoint, Tableau, Prezi, Keynote, or any other kind of presentation software. If you are someone that's seeking a way to make a case or deliver information to your audience effectively, then this book is for you.

What Is STC?

Now that we understand why stories are so powerful and necessary, let's take a closer look at what STC is. STC can be thought of as a language in and of itself. Unlike most languages though, it's fairly easy and quick to learn, so long as you use the right methodology. The problem is no one has been able to simplify STC in a way that allows it to be taught to others easily. Until now. The methodology that I developed makes teaching, learning, and becoming proficient in STC a simple process. Divided into five steps, this process has been tested out, put into practice, and refined many times over the course of a decade, until it evolved into the state that it's in now. My research and experience have shown me that if someone were to try learning STC without using this methodology, it would take them two years to attain proficiency and five years to become an advanced learner. With this methodology though, that same person could attain proficiency in STC in just a few hours, so long as they give their full attention to what they're learning.

Research indicates that individuals who speak more than one language are twice as likely than people who only speak one language to retain their normal cognitive functioning after they've suffered a stroke (Hope et al., 2015). Put in layman's terms, this means that bilingual people are more likely than monolingual people to make a successful recovery after having a stroke. This is because bilingual people have more neural connections in their brains. When they suffer a stroke, some of those connections, which are highways where thoughts are carried across, are destroyed. Having more neural connections, then, means having more highways left after some are destroyed, making it easier for the brain to keep functioning as it used to. Similarly, learning new languages can protect against other neurological conditions, such as Alzheimer's and dementia (Anderson et al., 2020). Having learned five different languages, I can objectively say that learning STC was akin to learning a sixth language. Before I developed my methodology for it, it certainly was just as hard as learning a new language as well. That becoming bilingual and learning STC have this similarity means that STC could have similar cognitive benefits to bilingualism. It doesn't mean, however, that STC should be quite as difficult to learn. There should be a much simpler and faster way of teaching and understanding it clearly. Luckily, now there is.

Language and STC Analogy

| | Language Analogy | | | | STC Equivalent | |
Level	Description	Lemmas	Grammar	STC	Experience
Level 1	Basic communication	100	None	3	Rookie
Level 2	Will help you speak a language in a day-to-day setting	800	Some	10	6 months
Level 3	Understand dialogues in film or TV	3,000	Structure	20	2 years
Fluent	Read and understand a novel and news articles	8,000	Advanced	20	5 years
Native	Native speaker	15,000+	Native	20	10+ years

The existing and commercially available methods of teaching STC primarily focus on charts, because charts are the easiest visuals to learn. These charts show their audiences simple ways of translating things like grammar, structure, and syntax to effective visuals that form meaningful sentences. These sentences then come together in those charts to create meaningful stories. The problem with this methodology is that it forces the learner to rapidly use several tools and frameworks at once while trying to improve their STC skills. This can cause them to become overwhelmed and lead to some degree of confusion. As a result, mastering STC can take longer than it should. That the creators of this methodology have overlooked this problem is understandable. After all, they're all either visual artists and copywriters who are writing books, creating training modules or giving expert advice on STC. None of them are practitioners of STC and have a background in strategy consulting. Instead, they're the kind of people you'd hire to draft a design or pretty up existing charts. This means that these individuals that usually teach STC aren't real practitioners of this language nor are they the ones that create decks that end up being worth millions of dollars. That being the case, is it any wonder that STC has been difficult to teach and learn up till now?

Unlike other methods of teaching STC, the methodology you'll encounter in this book teaches you a comprehensive suite of skills rather than just one dimension of those skills the way other methods erroneously do. It also teaches you those skills in the proper order, again contrary to the other methodologies out there. In doing so, this book will show you 16 chart families are all you need to gain proficiency in STC and this book gives the tools you require to master their use. These words and charts are what make up your STC vocabulary. Once you've learned them, you'll be able to move on to how to structure them properly. Despite what others may have led you to believe, the core of STC is structure, just as the core of any language is grammar, as opposed to vocabulary. Knowing the right words obviously helps but if you don't know the correct grammatical rules, you won't be able to use those vocabulary words to communicate what you want. What you will gain from this book then, is a thorough understanding of how STC structures work. You'll then be able to couple that understanding with the vocabulary you learn. This way you'll have all you need to build a structure, fill in the blanks and thus tell a good story.

How and Why Most Methods, Books, Tutorials, and Courses Get This Wrong

If learning the structure of STC is so crucial, why do most of the materials out there get this so wrong? To understand this, we must first grasp how we got to this point. The world we live in today is enmeshed in an ever-growing ocean of data. The first drop in this ocean was web activities, which is a field that is experiencing exponential growth in and of itself. The endless growth of website and web activity has generated an exponential growth in data, with no real end in sight. This is because we generate data every time we place a phone call, buy a smartwatch, watch a video, go for a run, do an internet search, make a purchase or even walk by a security camera somewhere. Add to that the fact that we all have smartphones, social media accounts, RFID tags, GPS data, and more and it becomes clear to see that the ocean can only ever keep growing. It isn't just individuals that are adding to this though. It's companies as well, seeing as they are now converting their physical assets into digital ones, thereby creating digital reflections of themselves.

Today, many physical assets are surrounded by sensors and controllers which can pull a great deal of data from them. This is what happens when you purchase a new car, for instance. Millions of data points are created when you do something as simple as turning on the ignition and driving off.

This massive accumulation of multi-layered data is what's known as big data. Most companies and organizations aren't equipped to fully handle big data. It's simply too much for them to sort through, especially since a lot of the generated data simply isn't useful. This pool of "useless" data is typically left untouched. So far, it's estimated that only about 1% of companies have been able to figure out how to make some kind of use of them. Now, imagine that you're such a company. You have a massive amount of data in your hands and you need some way to visualize it. How do you go about doing this? A lot of companies try to do this by starting with the data. That right there is the problem because **storytelling by using data as your starting point is like trying to find a problem that fits the math problem you have.** This same logic applies to STC. If you start with the data—that is to say the vocabulary—then you will be scrambling around trying to find a structure that fits it. You might eventually be able to do so but it will take you much longer than it otherwise would have. You might also not be able to find the structure you need.

Of course, this problem of data doesn't just affect companies. It affects your visual storytelling abilities as well but raising the question, how do you go about identifying the right data to use and capturing them in charts? How do you go about visualizing them? True, charts aren't all about data. Text components and abstract concepts play an important part in storytelling with charts as well–more on that later. But they are an important part of charts. As such, the data issue poses unique questions and become unique problems for STC.

The thing about data is that it's there to support your headline message or claim, not the other way around. This is why using data as your starting point when telling a story is backward and difficult. Asking yourself the question, "I have a problem. What kind of data analysis do I need to do to figure out what's causing it?" on the other hand is not. This, in fact, is the right way to approach any problem. It's also the correct way to approach STC because STC is the only framework out there that will give you the exact tools you need to quickly develop a storyline. Once you have a storyline you can hone in on the chart that will lead you to the data you need.

Most of the materials out there covering STC teach it to you backward. They have you trying to find a problem that fits your solution, which is difficult. After all, if your solution is "11" that could be the answer to "10+1" or "5+6" or any other kind of equation. Now, let's go back to our previous language metaphor. Imagine that you want to ask someone for directions in a new language you're learning. What kind of mental strain do you think you would be in if you were expected to start recalling 100,000 vocabulary words before ever learning how you were supposed to string them together in a sentence. Do you think you would have any idea how to ask for directions in that case, even if you knew the words for "left" and "right?" How long would it take you to master that language, if this was the way you went about learning it?

The thing about storytelling is that it should come naturally to you, no matter what language you're using and what your proficiency level is. At least, so long as you know the necessary grammatical rules. The same logic applies to Storytelling with Charts. Considering this, it's vital that you suspend all that you think you know about STC as you venture further into this book. Only in doing so will you be able to develop a thorough understanding of the new language before you.

A Rule of Thumb Intuitive Approach

The aim of this book isn't just accelerating your language skills. It's also to equip you with the Rule of Thumb, otherwise known as "ROT" which you can use to actually "speak" the language you're learning. To that end, ROTs will be highlighted throughout the chapters and pages of this book. You will thus be able to remind yourself of these ROTs and refer back to them easily, if and when you need to. The ROTs are useful in that they help you to circumvent the steep learning curve that typically accompanies learning new languages, just as the rest of the book will.

To write an effective and educational book that actually achieves its aims, an author must be able to speak from a point of experience and firsthand knowledge. I possess both and am therefore able to share information and techniques with you that I know will be effective. I know, for example, that the scale you've been provided with above can help you to assess your storytelling skills. Once you've done that, you can begin working on how to tell better stories. As you'll see later on in this book, three different dimensions go into being able to tell the best stories. The ROTs you'll find in this book will help you to better navigate these dimensions, which will be explored in greater depth later on. As you navigate the different dimensions of storytelling, you will effectively become a better communicator without having to experience the struggles I personally went through in this regard. I've condensed more than two decades of hands-on experience into this book, after all, which have led to the development of a well-tested and the proven method you can now take advantage of.

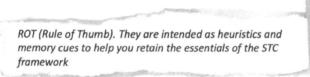

ROT (Rule of Thumb). They are intended as heuristics and memory cues to help you retain the essentials of the STC framework

My Struggle With Communication

I began my career working in corporate America, working in General Electric (GE), which at the time was one of the most valuable, not to mention largest companies in the world. As part of my job, I had to do weekly presentations, using charts. My career and professional growth depended on my ability to effectively communicate the work I had been doing to my superiors through these presentations. In the initial years of my career, I struggled a lot with this communication method, even though I developed excellent turnaround plans and worked hard on product launches. The training that we were given on how to prepare presentations was ineffective. While I could make presentations comfortably, my slides were, objectively speaking, disastrous. I was unable to translate all the hard work, great findings, and accomplishments I had made into an easily understandable format. But I wasn't the only one struggling with this. STC has never been a corporate forte, which meant that my superiors didn't know how to provide me with useful feedback on how I could improve my presentations.

It wasn't until later, when I had gone into management consulting, that I started to learn how STC was supposed to be done and began to get better at it. I hit another bump in the road, though, when I got to a position where I was managing others, seeing as I now had to teach them how to do slides. This was one of the biggest struggles I ever faced. It took newcomers to STC a very long time to master this communication method, even after countless training sessions and projects. This was doubly problematic for me as it prevented me from focusing on higher-level stuff.

Unfortunately, most colleges and universities don't prepare you to deliver real-world professional and corporate presentations. Given that, it's no wonder that I spent so much of my time working on presentations instead of doing my actual work. When working on presentations, a lot of people don't realize that there's an art and story-building quality to it. It is not just about charts and graphs nor is it solely about finding the right data and figures to back those charts up. Sometimes you need to use various creative methods to make and prove a point in a presentation. This is something that many rookies, and even I myself, initially overlooked when working on presentations. We essentially forgot that we needed to use both data and abstractions to design and build compelling stories that would captivate our audience, rather than bore them during our presentations.

My promise to you in writing this book is that you will not have to struggle with the same thing once you're through with it. It's also that you'll be proficient in STC in less than a day once you have finished reading it. This is because this book is a two-in-one kind of work. It is a book and workbook rolled into one. Thus, it makes you think and practice what you learn even as you keep reading. This is why you'll come across various charts and graphs that illustrate what you have read at certain points in the book. Seeing these charts after reading portions of the book will help you see how you can translate written information into visual stories.

The thing to remember about storytelling is that it never serves just a single purpose, regardless of who your audience is. When you're doing a promotion what you're trying to do is both convey a message and convince your audience of it. A good story can accomplish both of these things because it has the power to move the hearts and minds of audiences. It can motivate people to take action on whatever it is you want them to commit to. You have probably experienced this for yourself, when watching a good movie or reading a book, listening to someone give a speech, or watching TV. The emotional impact of a written and oral story is delivered through the words that it uses. When you're giving a presentation, charts have the ability to do the exact same thing that words can. They can have the same kind of impact, if you know how to use them. Otherwise, your presentation can come across as boring, confusing, or dull.

The approach that will be discussed in this book is one that is sure to work for any kind of audience. You can have the kind of emotional impact you want to have on anyone, regardless of industry and background, using STC as it's covered in this book. Once you've finished reading, you'll have to put what you have learned to practice. In doing so, you'll be able to become more advanced and proficient in STC in just a short amount of time.

The examples and case studies you'll encounter in this book are neither fictitious nor are they secondhand stories. They are all experiences that I have faced throughout my professional career as a client-facing strategy consultant. In my line of work, I've faced countless challenges, none of which are specific to any type of industry. In other words, they're the kinds of challenges that you yourself may have faced or may come to face in the future.

Many of the books found on the market today, focusing on this subject, are designed to teach how to tell single-message stories. Though this is a simpler process to master, it doesn't convey the full picture those wanting to learn STC need to see. Most books on this topic tend to be one dimensional, in contrast, STC is a three-dimensional subject in and of itself. This is something Storytelling With Charts recognizes. Therefore, it is the only book currently in the market to offer a more in-depth understanding of it.

Thus far, I have created and pitched presentations to individuals, leaders, and audiences from all walks of life, from kings to heads of state, CEOs and board members, and to senior public officials and executive committees. To protect these individuals' right to privacy and out of respect for them, a number of client names, locations, and some specific details have been changed throughout this book. Some details have been omitted as well. The presentations I've given to these different kinds of people have ranged from strategies to proposal pitches. The process I've outlined in this book is therefore the culmination of more than two decades' worth of hand–on experience. The following pages, then, contain all the things I've learned and come to refine through these experiences.

My idea in writing Storytelling With Charts is to take the science of what I've learned in managing consulting and bring it to life by combining it with the art of direct response marketing and behavioral science. Direct response marketing is a type of marketing strategy that encourages consumers to immediately respond to the messages they're receiving. Behavioral science, on the other hand, is the scientific study of human behavior. Merging these two studies with STC creates a powerful storytelling tool that can ethically hijack and captivate your audience toward your ultimate presentation goal.

In the coming chapter, you will encounter numerous concepts of direct response marketing and behavioral science. One concept that you will encounter is the Lindy Effect. The Lindy Effect, which will be examined more closely in the coming chapters, is a phenomenon where some things age in reverse. Perishable goods with expiration dates, for instance, experience the Lindy Effect. You will see how such concepts can be used to strengthen the story you're telling during presentations. The fact is, you can't just use colorful charts and technology to tell a story. Such things can add to stories and make aesthetic improvements upon them but not be the whole of the story.

Though you might think STC is going to be a complicated thing to learn before you sit down to learn it, the general concepts behind the STC framework haven't changed drastically for over a century. This process, supplemented by various scientific concepts, can easily help you connect the dots between data points, weave a logical structure between them and create a compelling story that flows flawlessly.

I got the idea to write this book and show readers like you how to do this one day, when I was working on archiving all my intellectual property. While sorting through the materials before me, I couldn't help but notice the more than 20,000 strategy decks I'd either created, co-created, or reviewed at some point throughout my career in the past two decades. Of course, I owed my team great thanks for helping me to reach this milestone, seeing as I couldn't have made them all from scratch. A number of them had to be created from scratch though, especially during those early years of my career. Looking through these materials, I couldn't help but recall all the trial and error I'd gone through, the continuous feedback I had gotten from clients, the audiences I was presenting to, and the partners of the firms I was a part of. They all played an important part in helping me to master my skill, which I now had the urge to pass on to others.

The process I followed in creating decks is the same process that will be outlined in this book. Naturally, it has been refined and improved upon over the years. Now, it's in such a state that a newcomer to STC can use it to hit the ground running. The desire to give newcomers this ability was part of the reason why I decided to write *Storytelling With Charts*. Another reason is that the struggle I went through when working with technical experts was fresh on my mind. Throughout my career I worked closely with some of the world's leading experts in various fields, sometimes leading a consortium of technical firms, other times retaining subject matter and technical expertise. The insights provided by these experts were always crucial to the work that I was doing. But structuring all that information was never those experts' forte, at least not that I could see. One of the tasks that any strategy consultant has to undertake is to take the insights they're given and put them into a cohesive story.

Storytelling is a hard-to-learn skill in the corporate world, especially if you've never worked as a strategy consultant before. Client-facing strategy consultants spend more than half their time designing, building, creating, and reviewing decks. That's a tremendous amount of time since they usually work 80+ hour weeks. They spend another significant portion of their time making presentations to CEOs and even various world leaders. In doing so, they get to practice their storytelling, critical thinking, and presentation skills far more than people in other industries and positions do. When they're not doing that, they're actively collecting data, conducting interviews, holding meetings, making analyses, and more to find the content they need to support their decks. What's more, the more a strategy consultant rises in seniority, the more presentations they end up having to make, not less. One very simple conclusion can be drawn from this fact: if a strategy consultant is not or cannot become a good storyteller, their career won't advance very far.

So, why aren't storytelling skills taught to people going into strategy consulting more? You might think the reason for this is that strategy consulting is a secretive industry by its very nature. But let's face it, in the internet age, nothing's really as big a secret as it used to be some two decades ago. The real reason these skills aren't more widely taught is actually rather disappointing: no one has ever come up with or bothered to come up with a good method of teaching them effectively and quickly to others. They haven't been able to do so because storytelling feels like it's too customized and like it cannot be systemized. That, however, is simply not true, as you will discover in the coming chapters, as this book will provide you with a working system and train your heuristic.

That word may have caught you aback a bit. That's reasonable as it comes from the Ancient Greek word Eureka. Eureka is a very simple procedure that can help you find adequate, though often imperfect, answers to difficult questions. Training your heuristic, then, means developing your ability to find innovative answers to challenging questions. In providing you with this training, Storytelling With Charts, will prove that STC is actually a simpler process than you probably thought it was. Because the core of creating individual charts is building the narrative and story you'll be telling. You may choose an approach that works best for you to create a horizontal and landscape-oriented presentation filled with charts. But by the end of this book, you'll be able to easily convert that to a vertically oriented portrait document by adding to the narrative and elaborating on the messages you were already giving. Learning all this will make switching between reports and presentations simple, which should be a relief to hear if you're far more used to writing reports than making presentations.

The good thing about horizontal presentations is that you can apply their inherent logic to any other form of storytelling, from reports and books to podcasts and videos. The only tricky part about switching mediums like this is data. Moving one format to another, you might feel like you're getting overwhelmed by all the data you have to manage. Sifting through all that unnecessary data that we had discussed earlier and finding those bits of information that you really need, which make up about 1% of what you have, can certainly be overwhelming. Luckily, this is something this book will help you with as well.

In today's day and age, we are constantly bombarded with data from all directions. Meanwhile, our attention spans have been shrinking continually over the years. Our average attention span was 15 seconds in 2000. In 2015, it had dropped to 8.25 seconds, according to one study, meaning that we now have shorter attention spans than goldfish (Hayes, 2022). This is problematic because it has made holding our audience's attention during the presentation has become even more challenging and stressful. Thanks to the rise of fake news and misinformation, it's as if we have become immune to being given information and treat it with skepticism. Being able to hold the audience's attention and inform them in the way we want during presentations requires recognizing all this. It requires building, designing, and structuring presentations in a way that directly addresses these issues.

Presenters who don't recognize these facts end up committing major mistakes in their presentations and losing their audience's attention as a result. One common mistake they make is to start a presentation with the end result or conclusion. This takes away from the emotional drive of the story they're telling. It causes them to lose the emotional trigger they could have used to keep people engaged. A good way to avoid making such mistakes is to think of every chart you have to use in your story as a problem you're trying to solve. All of those problems are part of a larger problem. To solve the larger problem, you have to address the smaller ones first. Einstein has said, "If I had an hour to solve a problem, I'd spend the first 55 minutes asking the right questions..." (Debevoise, 2014). This is what you need to do to create stories with charts as well.

An added challenge of STC is that we all have different worldviews and points of view. This means that you'll often find yourself in a position where you're making a presentation to someone who holds very different beliefs and views from yours. This might make you think you'll have a tough time connecting with your audience and getting your message across. But the thing is these differences aren't actually relevant to your presentation. What is relevant is your goal, which is to craft your messaging in such a way that you can get people from all sorts of different backgrounds and belief systems to become invested in it. Being able to achieve this marks the difference between success and failure in storytelling with charts. If you aren't able to tell your story well, then whatever valuable insights you possess as an expert in your field will, unfortunately, go to waste, along with your hard work. Well-crafted messages, though, can prevent that from ever being the case.

By the end of this book, you will be able to master all of these different skills and thus master the art and science of storytelling with charts.

Once you master the skills outlined in this book, you'll become a one-in-a-million storyteller, no matter what subjects you're creating a presentation on. Overall, *Storytelling With Charts* will help you to master five tactics: persuasion tactics like the bubble, the art of storytelling with a specific focus on the hero's journey, horizontal logic, systems thinking, and critical thinking.

A final device *Storytelling With Charts* will help you make use of is dual thinking, which assumes that there can be only two contrasting, mutually exclusive realities or choices (Chamberlain, 2019). Dual thinking was initially created by William James, an American philosopher and the first psychological educator in the country. Dual thinking is also a process that takes place in our brains. Our brains are essentially lazy and like processing easy information, so long as it doesn't trigger our brain's BS detector. Given these preferences, having STC start with a lazy brain and then having your logical brain keep the ongoing story in check would be the best, most engaging strategy to follow. In doing so, you can craft truly engaging stories using charts.

Having said all that, it should be noted that this book is not a tutorial on how to use platforms like Microsoft PowerPoint, Apple KeyNote, Prezi, or Google Presentation. While knowing how to use these platforms can help. But the fact is you can hire people nowadays for $20 an hour to put your designs on one of these platforms themselves. You can also download plugins like Thinkcell if you want to do your presentation without hiring anyone. The real difficulty that comes with STC doesn't lie in using things like PowerPoint. Rather it lies in designing storylines and making charts that could support them adequately. A trick you can use to pick up the pace is to create a template you can use for your presentations that reflects your brand, which will be discussed in greater delta n Chapter 3. After that, you can let the plugins run the process for you.

As a final note, it's important that you do not skip any portion of this book but rather read it all. All in all, it will take you less than a day to get through *Storytelling With Charts*, seeing as it has plenty of visuals. That means you only need to spend four hours to invest in a skill that will serve you forever.

How I Structured This Book

Before you proceed, I want to take a beat and give you the bad news first. You're not going to become an expert at STC the moment you finish reading the final page of this book. However, you will be able to gain proficiency in a week or even a day, depending on how quickly you finish this book and how attentively you read it. To gain proficiency quickly, you should practice what you learn as you read this book. You should remember that anything that promises you instant proficiency in any skill is likely a scam. The only way to gain proficiency in something is to use standardized tools, systems, and frameworks, like the ones that will be outlined herein.

So, what will the process of gaining proficiency look like in this book? *Storytelling With Charts* follows a very simple sequence. The first part of the book will teach you the vocabulary you need to know. The second will help you to order those vocabulary words in comprehensible sentences. The third part will show you how to put those sentences together to create a flowing, engaging narrative.

The content that each chapter will discuss will not be summed up or explained at the beginning of the chapters. Doing that would be removing the emotional trigger of the story being told in *Storytelling With Charts*. As such, it's important that you do not skip ahead while reading. Otherwise, you won't be able to learn how to walk before you try running and even flying. The good news is that while this book is a tutorial, it's not a dull one. In writing *Storytelling With Charts* I've tried to make it as interesting and entertaining as possible. That said, some of the concepts discussed here, such as critical thinking and logic, might be a bit on the duller side for some readers. Given that, I've tried to keep the sections of the book discussing such things as brief as humanly possible. You don't need to know all the detailed mathematics that go into storytelling, after all, but you do need to understand its basic approach and background, so that it'll stick in your mind the first time you read it. To make sure that that happens, I've tried to paint a picture of the various concepts explored in this chapter, so that you can relate to the different aspects of the story more easily. Try to link the concepts and stories and the concepts will become that much more vivid and therefore memorable for you.

If you remain skeptical, then consider this. During training the sessions I give, there's this experiment I always run. In the experiment, I distribute a short case study before training begins. I then break down participants into groups of five and ask them to build a short presentation. This serves two purposes. The first is to gauge where everyone is at skill and experience-wise. The second is to measure how much they've improved by the time the training is over. I accomplish this latter objective by asking participants, split into those same groups of five, to prepare another presentation on the same case studies at the end of the training. The participants thus re-do the work they had done at the beginning. The differences between the two presentations often end up being astounding. Whatever score they had gotten in their "before" presentations usually rise to something between eight to ten after less than one day of training. The things I teach those participants in my training sessions are no different than what I will be teaching you in this book. That being the case, are you ready to begin your "training" as well and reap the same rewards.

The Companion Toolkit

To complement your learning, an optional toolkit is available that provides helpful supplemental resources. This toolkit includes a video tutorial for audio-visual reinforcement of key concepts. You'll also gain access to exclusive resources like cheat sheets, templates and presentations to help put your new skills into practice. With these materials at your fingertips, you can accelerate your proficiency in just a few hours of focused learning. The toolkit is designed to be a valuable supplement for those looking to master the framework efficiently. Please consider this additional option if you wish to optimize and expand upon the core content covered in this book.

You can access the toolkit by going to:

www.storytellingwithcharts.com/toolkit

Chapter 1: STC—An Introduction and General Framework

We can be blind to the obvious, and we are also blind to our blindness. – Daniel Kahneman

When escaping a war-torn country, I had to flee on a boat, because the airport was being shelled. My ultimate destination was Germany, a country whose language I could not speak. I was only 17 at the time and I chose Germany because I had an uncle living there, who I thought would be able to help me get on my feet. When I arrived, though, he told me the best thing I could do right now was to go back home, since Germany was in the midst of a recession. But going back to be shelled during the day and staying in too-fragile bunkers at nights was not an option. I knew I somehow had to earn my college degree. Otherwise, I would end up being drafted into some militia, where I would be grievously injured, maimed, or worse, killed off. The burden of putting myself through college was on me as my parents could cover neither my living expenses nor my tuition. This meant I needed to find a job. Since I didn't speak German, I had to find the kind of job where I only needed to speak a handful of words to make do. So, it was that I went on a job hunting spree to find some kind of waiting position in a nightclub, somewhere that was so loud nobody would want me to speak too much anyways. The kind of job that gifted me with a lifelong case of intermittent tinnitus, which I struggle with to this day.

To make a very long story short, I did manage to find a position at the most popular nightclub in town, where I became good friends with the DJ. He was the main reason for the club's popularity. Once we grew closer, I couldn't help but ask him how he was able to keep such a diverse and large crowd so engaged with his music. What was his secret? My friend plainly said that he couldn't possibly please everybody, no matter what he played. So, what he tried to do was rotate and diversify his playlist as fast as he could. That way, if 30% of the crowd loved a song he played, then the next 30% would end up loving the following song and the one after that would be for the remaining third of the crowd. If he noticed that the crowd wasn't into a certain song, then he had to find a way to switch to another quickly and seamlessly. But it wasn't just about pleasing everyone in the crowd. He also had to keep them engaged. Luckily, he had developed certain tactics for this. For instance, he would put on songs that had become classics, so that the audience would know the words enough to sing along. Then he would lower the volume and let them take the mic, so to speak. He would play the first part of a song lyric and then let the crowd finish the rest:

"To do so, I have several tactics, for example, I put classic songs for which they know the lyrics, and lower the volume to let them sing it out loud. I let the first sentence of the first lyric play out loud, then turn the volume down to allow the crowd to sing the rest."

I learned two very important lessons from my DJ friend, especially since there were several elements at play in the strategy he employed, including anticipation, surprise, and rewards. These elements worked together to create a memorable experience for his audience and motivate them to take action. Though this anecdote did teach me plenty, I would be lying if I claimed that the lessons I learned from it taught me how to design effective presentations. That I, unfortunately, had to learn the hard way. It took me over a decade to develop and improve my skills, as well as a continuous process of trial and error, coupled with countless books and one-on-one coaching sessions with my superiors during strategy and consulting years. Yet this is the story that I refer to every time I review a story deck because it serves as a vivid reminder of the process I can now practice in my sleep.

A key takeaway from this anecdote is that if you're making a presentation to more than just one person, you will not be able to please every single audience member. Instead, you'll have to keep playing different tunes so that you can cater to everyone while keeping your audience as engaged as possible. As you'll go on to discover later on, though you may have a general idea about your audience's background going into a presentation, you'll never know what everyone's specific backstory is. If you try to tailor your stories for everyone's specific background and tune them to their liking, you'll only end up losing valuable time.

I wasn't drawn to the field of consulting because of my own, personal background. Going into the business, I didn't know that consultants spent the majority of their time working on slide decks. I started out my career despising charts and my engineering background was of no help to me in this regard. I wanted to go and build stuff, after all, not spend my time stuck before a computer, working on slide after slide. Regardless, I struggled for years, wasting countless hours trying to perfect those slides. True, my math, engineering, and computer science background did help me conduct my analyses and develop good insights. But most of that hard work ended up going to waste because I couldn't communicate them through meaningful stories.

The first charts I ever created were a complete disaster, at least compared to the ones that I'm able to make today. Though they were quite sophisticated, it was impossible for my audience to understand them. This is because I didn't spare a thought to my audience as I worked on my beautiful, colorful charts. One of the directives I was initially given was that I shouldn't create too many slides. I heard that statement and understood it to mean "Cram as much information as you possibly can on a single slide." As a result, I ended up working on a dashboard that basically described a new story on every chart and slide.

This might sound nonsensical to you, hearing it as an outsider. But you'd be surprised just how many veteran strategy consultants, high up in the corporate ladder follow the exact same logic. This is a pitfall for many consultants, particularly when they have to make a presentation to busy world leaders, wrap everything up in 20 minutes and still leave enough time over for a 10-minute Q&A. Consultants that stumble onto this pitfall try to cram all their findings into five to 10 executive summaries, meaning they spend an average of two to five minutes on every slide.

The goal of a presentation is to persuade your audience of something, be that an idea, a message, or a sales pitch. As a ROT, persuasion cannot be achieved through long-winded speeches and presentations. "Less is more" is the rule that reigns supreme in the art of persuasion, as well as in the art and science of storytelling. This is why author Kevin Dutton considers brevity to be one of the four key factors to persuasion in his book Split–Second Persuasion (Dutton, 2010). Brevity, or simplicity as Dutton puts it, can ensure key ideas stick in the audience's minds. In a word, it makes your presentation more memorable.

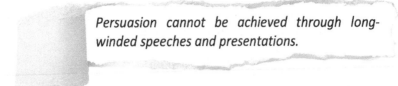

Persuasion cannot be achieved through long-winded speeches and presentations.

That said, mastering the art of brevity requires knowing more, not less, and thus mastering the art of storytelling itself. The more you know, the more you'll be able to uncover the creative and engaging ways you can use the toolkits at your disposal. At the same time, you'll be able to improve your storytelling heuristic, until it becomes second nature to you. Over time, storytelling heuristic you'll find that you longer have to put yourself under any mental strain to make use of this skill, as it has become as natural to you as speaking. This will increase your confidence in your STC skills, which, as it happens, is another key factor of persuasion, right alongside empathy and self–interest. But more on that later: For now, let's focus on how the STC relates to the mechanics of our brains and decision-making capabilities, to better understand the role that genuine brevity plays in it. Let's take a closer look at how our brains operate and make decisions and how basic brain mechanisms influence the way we hear and see the world, since STC deals directly with visual and aural information and how these can be communicated to your audiences' brains.

The Dual Process Theory

I lived in Saarbrücken, a city bordering France, in my first year of college. Here I used to support myself by working as a bartender and waiter at a club. Throngs of French customers would flock to the club from across the border. My roommate, Michael, and I used to offer to let these French customers sleep at our apartment after our shifts were over, if they missed the last bus to France and had nowhere else to stay. One of these customers was an astrologist and I can vividly remember discussing horoscopes with her. I remember her saying, "Horoscopes work and to prove it, I can guess both of yours. Yours is Gemini and Michael's is Cancer." The probability of her getting that right was one in 144 but get it right she did. This made me question my belief in horoscopes. I figured that maybe there was some truth to horoscopes after all, if she could guess our signs so accurately.

So, how did my brain process this information?

The dual process theory is a framework that psychologists and behavioral scientists use to describe how the brain's thinking processes work. The theory states that we can arrive at the same thought through two separate thought processes. One of these processes is conscious and explicit. The other is subconscious and explicit (Levine, 2017). One of these thought processes is slow, while the other is fast. One is emotional while the other is logical. You can probably guess which one is which. Before you do that, though, let's give some background on dual process theory. The point in doing this is not to cover the theory's entire history or give credit to its every contributor, but rather to give a general idea of its importance, the extensive research that has been conducted on it throughout the years, and show how the concept evolved into its current form, which neuroscientists believe humans use when they think and make decisions.

Dual process theory was originally attributed to William James (1842-1910), the American philosopher and the first educator in psychology. James studied epistemology—the theory of thought—and believed that the brain had two processes for thinking. He stated that one of these processes was empirical and was used when we were working on tasks such as designing something. The other, he went on, was based on our past experiences and was able to come up with abstractions as a result. In 1974, cognitive scientists Peter Wason and Jonathan Evans introduced the heuristic process and analytic process to the equation. The heuristic process allowed people to choose whatever information was relevant to their current situation and process them further, while discarding the excess. The analytic process takes the relevant information, selected by the heuristic process, and uses them to make decisions. In 1986, Richard E. Petty and John Cacioppo developed a model of persuasion, based on these theories. They posited that there were two ways to persuade others. One was for persuading people who were highly motivated at that moment. The other was for motivating people whose motivation levels were low. Highly motivated people tend to think carefully about whatever situation they're in, whereas people whose motivation levels are low don't. The latter group tends to be prone to taking shortcuts or making quick judgments. Hence the two different persuasion models.

In 1986, psychologist Steven Sloman added to the existing literature by introducing another interpretation of dual processing. He proposed that we have an associative thought process and a rule-based one. We use both these systems to make decisions. Our associative system makes decisions based on associations, like similarities. Hence the name. Our rule-based system uses symbolic content that has logical meaning to arrive at decisions (Sloman, 1986). Sloman suggested that our rule based system does not have total control over our actions. Instead, our associative system has some degree of control as well, seeing as it can suppress our rule-based system.

The psychologist Keith Stanovich went on to add to Sloman's theory and introduced these concepts in the book *Rationality and the Reflective Mind*. In this book, Stanovich broke down our rule-based thinking even further, into the reflective mind and algorithmic mind. The reflective mind is essentially able to consider things in the context of the bigger picture and thus understand the implications of an action or experience (Stanovich, 2011). The algorithmic mind, on the other hand, is able to get through a solution and clearly define the steps that need to be taken to reach a desired conclusion. In 2002, psychologist Daniel Kahneman built on these two theories that Stanovich had written about to create the Prospect Theory.

The Prospect Theory, which won Kahnemann the Nobel Prize, states individuals tend to be more motivated by the possibility of a loss, that is to say by losing out on something than they are by the possibility of gaining something (Kahneman & Tversky, 1979). In essence, Prospect Theory is a theory of choice and how we make our choices. Given that, it's widely used in behavioral economics and behavioral finance. The theory makes two key arguments:

- People are risk averse. They hate losing more than they actually like winning.
- People prefer definite gains to probabilistic gains.

In his book, *Thinking Fast and Slow*, Kahneman attributes these two behavioral preferences to the two ways in which our brain operates. He refers to these two ways as System 1 and System 2. System 1, Kahneman explains, is the lazy part of our brain. It's intuitive and uses associations and metaphors to get quick results and draft an understandable interpretation of reality. System 2 is the analytical part of our brain and uses analytical methods that require focus and effort to think through the choices in front of us to arrive at a decision.

To simplify matters, you can think of system 1 as your reptilian brain. The reptilian is the older of the two systems and is more instinctual and emotional, as you may have guessed from the very term "reptilian" which calls to mind an animalistic nature. Most of us aren't consciously aware of the things that our reptilian brain does. For instance, we don't really think about breathing. We don't have to. We just breathe. Our reptilian brain manages critical functions like that. It also regulates our attention and various emotions. It even manages our survival instincts, like fight or flight instinct which kicks in automatically when we sense a threat. All of this is data that our fast-thinking brains can process instantaneously. They do so because our lives, our literal survival, and well-being literally depend on it. In contrast, the other part of our brain works a lot more slowly. This part, earlier referred to as system 2, is responsible for making complex calculations and deep thinking.

As an ROT, you shouldn't make your presentation a one-sided brain activity. Instead, the presentation you work on should use both your reptilian brain and your logical brain. This way, it can appeal to your audience on multiple levels and be far more interesting and engaging for them.

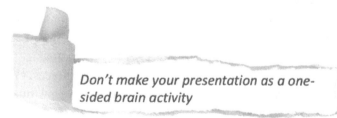

Don't make your presentation as a one-sided brain activity

Over the centuries there has been a lot of debate about which system is more dominant than the other during our decision-making processes. The truth is when one system becomes more dominant than the other depends on many factors. These factors include things like the situation at hand, the individual, the context, and more. What matters is that in the context of a large audience, we can safely assume that the two systems are working together, affecting how that audience arrives at the conclusions they arrive at and the decisions they make. It's important to know these two systems in STC, then, because when you're making a presentation you're effectively trying to convince your audience of something. You're trying to get them to make a certain decision, which may be to buy something you're selling, choose your pitch over those of others, or believe a point you're trying to make. When you know how your audience's decision-making processes work, you can structure the story you're telling in a way that engages them directly.

We distinguish between two types of dual thinking processes in this book. The first is the distinction between the lazy and the more intuitive brain. The second is the more logical brain or System 1 and System 2 as Kahneman called them. This book also discusses the left brain and the right brain. Though this is not really how the brain works, the left and right brains are typically used to refer to rational and emotional thinking mechanisms respectively. As such, going forward these two thinking mechanisms will be referred to as the left brain and right brain and will sometimes be used interchangeably with System 1 and System 2. In doing so, the book will be making a distinction between cognitive biases and persuasion. When I use the terms System 1 and System 2, I will be discussing cognitive biases. When I use the terms left brain and right brain, though, I'll be discussing the matter of persuasion. With that out of the way, let's take a closer look at how dual process theory works and affects decision-making within the context of STC.

The Importance of Influence, Decision-Making Skills, and Taking Action

The key takeaway here is that you should never assume anything about your audience. As such, you shouldn't make your presentation into a one-sided brain activity. Instead, take the safe approach and address both System 1 and System 2, seeing as they are the processes that are responsible for decision-making in humans. In order for a message to succeed in persuading someone of something, it needs to address both System 1 and System 2, since they are the processes that are responsible for decision-making. When you're telling a story, your messaging should target System 1 while supplying the audience with continuous emotional triggers and engaging content as frequently as possible. In doing so it can become truly powerful, captivating, and memorable.

As I'll discuss in greater detail later, when you set out to develop a presentation, you start out with a specific goal or objective in mind. If you don't have one, you need to establish one quickly, before you begin working on your presentation. But more on how to do that later. Once you have established your goal, you move onto presenting your big idea to your audience. This big idea is what you want your audience to accept by the time you're finished with your presentation. Suppose you need to write a message that you want your audience to believe. Your message will be true, but that is not necessarily enough for people to believe that it is true. However, cognitive ease is only one of several ways we can use to improve believability, which we'll discuss later, in greater detail. That means that if you care about being thought credible and intelligent, you should use simple language and make it memorable. As one study shows, deliberately using complex vocabulary to make an argument seem more convincing or intelligent, usually proves to be an ineffective strategy. Using easy to grasp vocabulary, on the other hand, doesn't see as it makes concepts immediately graspable for the audience (Oppenheimer, 2006).

When you're building a nonfiction story, what you're trying to do is to take your audience through a journey, going from point A—your starting point to point B—the conclusion you want your audience to arrive at. In other words, you are trying to lead your audience to somewhere specific, with your overall goal in mind.

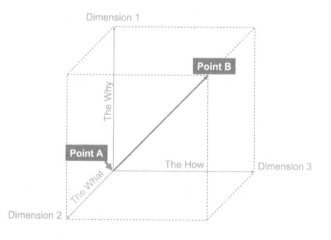

To accomplish this, you will need to take steps during your presentation to influence your audience. This is the fundamental of storytelling.

The idea of STC is to supply you with the tools you need to take your audience from Point A to point B effectively. Point A can be considered a variable. This is because it can be difficult to establish at times, seeing as the members making up your audience are different from one another. But the thing is, you don't need to know any real specifics about your audience to tell them a story. What you need to do is establish the universal aspects of your audience. You cannot understand the beliefs and characteristics of every person making up your audience, after all. Since you can't do that, you need to create the kind of story that can speak to them all on some level. This is why another ROT to make note of is that you need to establish your presentation goal and strategic objectives without wasting too much time on understanding your audience.

The goal of the STC system is not to present a work of fiction to your audience the way a novel or Hollywood story would. Unlike such fics, its purpose and goal are something other than providing pure entertainment. It's to influence a group, regardless of what backgrounds its individual members come from, using your persuasion skills. Its endpoint—point B—arrives with you essentially asking your audience for something.

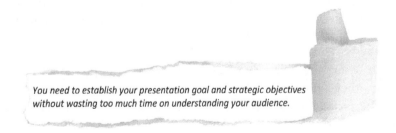

You need to establish your presentation goal and strategic objectives without wasting too much time on understanding your audience.

Whatever it is you are asking for, what you're trying to do with STC is persuade your audience to:
- Change their minds about something.
- Believe in your new findings.
- Take action to purchase something from you.
- Fund your venture.

- Give you their support.
- Change their views.
- Change their beliefs.
- Take action on something.
- Like your presentation.
- Accept and admire your work.

Considering all the different things you might be asking for from your audience in STC, understanding the science of influence is essential. This understanding can help you craft the right messages, which will drive the analysis you're doing and the content you're creating. You will then be able to pull all of this together in a convincing story.

Strategic Objectives of Traditional Storytelling Techniques

Your strategic objectives are the main purposes of the story you're telling. This can be your sales pitch, a problem-solving solution, a proposal, a direct response, new findings, or some such similar thing.

Your strategic objectives fall into one of two categories, regardless of what they may be. These are Category 1 and Category 2. Category 1 is made up of strategic objectives that are asking your audience to give you something so that they can get something in return. Category 2 is made up of strategic objectives that are asking your audience to believe in something or recognize you as the authority of something. This means that such objectives aim to have your audience give you credibility or recognition for something that you have done.

Though your strategic objectives may change depending on what category they fall into, your main goal will never change, as you will always be asking your audience to act on something or other. This is why every story harbors an element of persuasion in STC. It's also why you need to work on achieving your strategic objectives so that you can achieve your overall goal.

Story Type	Category 1	Category 2	Giving to You	Receiving from You
Problem Solution	✓	✓	Change the status quo to solve a problem	Solution to a problem
Investment Pitch	✓		Cash investment	Expected return on investment
Findings Report		✓	Credibility	Knowledge
Performance Report		✓	Credibility	Insights
Proposal	✓	✓	Contract	Products or services
Sales Pitch	✓		Cash payment	Products or services

The Three-Dimensional Framework (3DF) of STC

As discussed previously during dual process theory, we make decisions through the dual processes that operate within our brains. For your audience to decide to believe your story, you have to tell a convincing one. Hence, if you want to tell a convincing story and persuade your audience of something then you need to appeal to both the logical and intuitive sides of the brain. This is because people's emotions affect their decision-making processes just as much as their logic and reasoning capabilities, if not more so. The STC technique that is able to accomplish this is called the three-dimensional framework (3DF). As you might have guessed from the name, it is built on three core elements, no matter what kind of story you're telling: emotions, logic, and engagement. Think of these three dimensions as the three crucial ingredients in a combustion engine. All three ingredients need to be present in the engine. Otherwise, the engine will not work.

Dimension	Engine Metaphor	Metaphoric Purpose	Real Purpose
Emotion	Spark	To trigger the spark that lights the gas	Calls on intuitive and cognitive ease to strengthen influence and power or ignite persuasion
Logic	Gas	The fuel that keeps the engine running.	Acts as a guide for the required synthesis and analytical processes and provides the credibility, rationale, and proof that all given claims and hypotheses need
Engagement	Oil/Lubricant	The lubricant that prevents friction and prolongs the engine's life	Keeps the audience in a state of anticipation, ensures retention and captivates them

Emotions, logic, and engagement serve both metaphoric purposes and real purposes, as can be seen from the above chart. They work together to keep the engine running and keep you from losing your audience. As an ROT, think of these three dimensions as a sort of litmus test. When you're working on a presentation, ask yourself if the story you're telling works on all three levers. If it doesn't, then you run the risk of losing your audience.

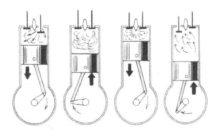

Influence is something that works from the bottom up, with each dimension playing a crucial part in nudging your audience in the direction you want them to go.

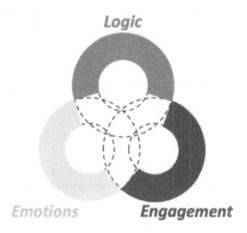

Logic

Emotions   Engagement

The term for the first of these dimensions, emotions, comes from the Latin word "movere" meaning to move. Emotions are one of the primary forces of the brain, energizing behavior. They also influence our mood. The second dimension, logic, is how our brain validates and confirms the copious amount of information that it receives. It uses cognitive resources to mediate the responses we give to emotions, whenever they're triggered or called forth by System 1. The third and final dimension, engagement, retains the audience's attention during a presentation or gets them to pay attention in the first place. In this day and age, engagement can be thought of as a currency. People have a limited supply of "attention" and have become increasingly conditioned to expect to receive a reward in exchange for giving you their attention. Engagement is just as important a dimension as emotions and logic because if your audience isn't listening to you, then they aren't able to absorb the content you're giving them anyways.

Going back to logic, this dimension actually serves two different purposes, as you saw in the previous chart. The first is to guide you as you identify relevant data and synthesize them, so that you'll have proof on hand that can support your hypotheses and claims. This will provide you with the framework you need to solve problems, as you'll see later. The second is to use the data you've obtained and the analyses you've made to structure an easy-to-understand visual that can back your claims.

An ROT to remember when thinking about these three dimensions is that the story you're creating has to be based on logic and structured logically but it should be strategically enhanced with emotional and engaging content and cues, which can be used to influence and maintain engagement.

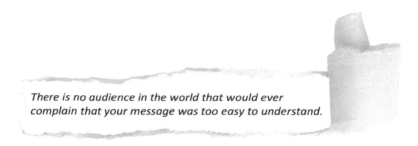

There is no audience in the world that would ever complain that your message was too easy to understand.

To understand how to use emotions as a vehicle for driving engagement, we must first understand emotions better. In 1980, psychologic Robert Plutchik, created something called the wheel of emotions. His intent in creating this wheel was to illustrate the many ways in which different emotions interact. The Plutchik wheel's basic idea is that there are eight primary emotions that can be broken down into two groups of positive and negative emotions (Buck & Oatley, 2007):

- Joy vs. Sadness
- Fear vs. Anger
- Anticipation vs. Surprise
- Disgust vs. Trust

According to the Plutchik wheel, various primary emotions add up to produce new ones. Love for instance arises as a combination of joy and trust. Guilt, on the other hand, is a combo of joy and fear. All of these resultant emotions have varying degrees of intensity.

When you're working on a presentation, there are specific kinds of emotions that you want to evoke and specific ones that you want to avoid. For instance, you don't want to cause your audience to grow bored, but you absolutely want to create a sense of trust. One way to go about evoking the emotions you want your audience to experience is by making use of mirror neurons. A neuron is a brain cell. Mirror neurons are a type of brain cells that perform an action on seeing someone else perform it (Winerman, 2021). The most obvious example of this is yawning when you see someone yawning.

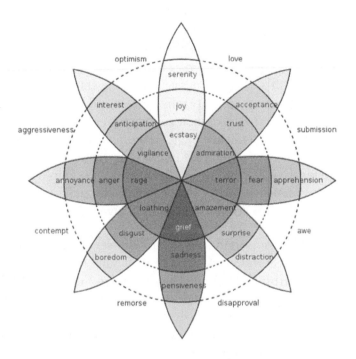

Another way to get your audience to emotionally respond to a story in the way that you want is to use polarization. Polarization happens when you let your audience experience something negative first and then relive it as a positive one. This is an effective reframing strategy to persuade people of a certain thing and evoke the kind of emotional response you want because our brains are hardwired to prioritize bad news over good news. Kahneman believes that this is an evolutionary quirk that came into being so that we could detect predatory threats early and thus ensure our survival (Kahneman, 2011). So, when you let your audience experience something negative before something positive, you work with the natural structure of the brain, not against it. If you're skeptical about this, consider the most basic form of stories: fairy tales. All fairy tales are structured the same way. There is a protagonist who goes on a journey, experiences something bad or challenging, then overcomes it. The bad thing that the protagonist goes through is the negative experience. The portion of the story where they overcome it is the positive framing for that story, which gets the reader even more invested in the story, as well as supportive of the protagonist's goals. This, right here, is what you're trying to achieve through polarization in STC.

Stories are a great way of building trust between you, as the storyteller, and your audience. Emotions not only add value to your story but also have the power to influence your listeners. Polarization is by far the most popular way of infusing stories with emotions, at least among copywriters. Experienced copywriters and fiction writers usually start out their stories with a negative message that triggers negative emotions. Then they follow that up with a positive message that triggers a positive emotion. In doing so, they take their audience on a negative to a positive journey that keeps the audience engaged and invested. They place their triggers within story arcs, which are useful tools that'll be explored more later. To achieve the same result, you need to employ the same polarization technique in STC, meaning that you need to start with a negative message and follow it up with a positive one.

That being said, it's important that your story starts with the truth and sticks to the truth. Stories work because they build trust. They won't be able to build any trust, though, if that stray from the truth. STC's goal isn't to present some fictional idea or scam to the audience. As such, using logic and rationale to chase after and present the truth in a cohesive narrative is vital. Luckily, we will explore all of the strategies you'll need to use to accomplish all this later on in the book.

Avoid Mistakes at All Costs

A colleague of mine, who I will refer to as John, was a smart and polished man that had an incredible pedigree. He had a promising career and was on the fast track to a partnership. John and I were working on a high-profile assignment, where we had to prepare a presentation due the next day. We had to submit the said presentation to our office before the morning arrived. So, we knew that we had to pull off an all=nighter and decided to order takeout.

The thing is, John had a bad case of the allergies and that night he struggled with a massively itchy nose, the kind of itch that wouldn't go away no matter how much time passed. John had told me about this that morning and took his hand to his nose to scratch the itch. Unfortunately, it was at that moment that another colleague of ours, Nancy, happened to walk by and saw what she thought was John, sitting there, picking his nose. She looked shocked but didn't say anything. She soon disappeared from sight, heading towards the opposite end of the office, where a work friend of hers was. The sound of their laughter was quick to reach us. Thereafter John became known as "the Pick," a nickname lifted from an episode title of Seinfeld. No matter what he did or tried, John couldn't shake the nickname off. Needless to say, he ended up quitting and moving to another city, where his reputation wouldn't chase after him.

The ROT learned from this lesson? Don't make so much as a single mistake. A single mistake is unfortunately enough to discredit your entire work and damage both your credibility and your presentation.

don't make a single mistake. One mistake can discredit your entire work, credibility or presentation

Paul Rozin is a psychologist who specializes in the science and study of disgust. In this study Rozin made the following observation:

"A teaspoon of sewage will spoil a barrel of wine, but a teaspoon of wine will do nothing for a barrel of sewage." (Rozin & Fallon, 1987)

What Rozin meant by this observation is that a negative incident and occurrence often outweigh positive ones. This is because our minds are predisposed to prioritize negative news and remember them more. This phenomenon is known as the negativity bias and is a remnant of our survival tactics from the stone age. Back then, human beings had to constantly be aware of external threats, like predators, and were therefore always on the lookout for them. Thus they, that is to say, became more likely to notice first and remember them more.

The research that Rozin conducted on this matter was corroborated in other studies that other academics went on to conduct and the findings of these studies were published in a paper entitled *Bad Is Stronger Than Good* (Baumeister et al., 2001). This paper outlines how things like bad emotions, bad parents, and bad feedback have a greater impact on our psyche than good ones. It also explains how bad information is processed more thoroughly than the good. The fact is the way our brains are wired means that positive impressions and stereotypes take longer to form. It also means that positive impressions and stereotypes can be refused more easily than negative ones. This is why avoiding mistakes at all costs when giving a presentation is essential. Otherwise a single mistake can negate all the claims that your presentation is making.

The Fallacy of the Complicated: Don't Act Like a Charlatan

When giving a speech at the Q1–2022 annual shareholders meeting at the Berkshire Hathaway, Warren Buffet referred to Wall Street financial advisors as worse than "monkeys" (Melloy, 2017). His exact words were "you can have monkeys throwing darts at the page and, you know, take away the management fees and everything, I'll bet on the monkeys over the advisors." Buffet went on to say, "It's amazing how hard people make what is a simple game. But of course, if they told everybody what a simple game it was, 90% of the income of the people that were speaking would disappear."

A common fallacy among business professionals is that creating and using complicated charts will help them gain credibility. This fallacy stems from the idea that if an analysis looks complicated, it has to be right. Though this assumption might be true to a certain extent and could work on some people, it backfired on those that use it more often than not. Take what happened as a result of the GameStock frenzy of 2021 as an example. For those of you that don't know, in January 2021, a number of WallStreetBets members decided to buy up and hold onto GameStop stock for a short period of time. In doing so, they could trigger what was known as a short squeeze. By January 20, the maneuver caused the company's stock prices to shoot up to nearly $40 per share. This meant that the share value had doubled in just three weeks. Five days later the price had gotten to 76$. On the morning of January 28th, it was $483.

This price increase meant that short-selling hedge funds suddenly found themselves dealing with significant losses. A week after the stocks reached their peak price about $36 billion was wiped off of its value, along with the four "meme" stocks that were being traded. As a result, those that were betting against GameStop suddenly found themselves facing $11 billion in year-to-date losses.

This happened on March 8th, 2020 but the story wasn't to end there. That same month, BCG filed a lawsuit against GameStop for $30 million for refusing to pay their consultancy fee. GameStop refused to pay this fee because it stated that BCG prioritized excessive fees over its clients' interests and because of the seemingly meager impact they had on the company's bottom line (Jones, 2021).

As a professional advisor myself, I have to confess that I am quite embarrassed about how this profession works and thus gives advisors a bad reputation, causing many of them to be stereotypes. The BCG lawsuit wasn't about GameStop's stock price and profits, after all. Rather it was about how BCG's contract's stated compensation was based on a variable fee based on a projected profit. More specifically, it was about the word "projected" as opposed to actual. The strategy consulting industry is renowned for making projections based on various complex models. However, these projections are rarely realized unless the client is actually able to implement them, which isn't always the case. The truth is some consultants use overly complex models as a method of ascertaining claims, even when the point or claim they're trying to prove isn't certain and shouldn't be treated as such. Given that, I say again that I understand the bad reputation the industry gets, as projections like these are responsible for it in the first place. Hence this story, while interesting on many levels, isn't all that surprising to me and to others.

I do not wish to get overly philosophical in this book and enter into an ethical debate on what's morally acceptable or not in the industry. I do have to make note of my own, personal preference, though, which is that it is better to not emulate the behaviors of a pretentious charlatan. In keeping with that, it's important that you create simple STC and make sure that the arguments and analyses you make in them remain simple as well.

Sadly, this is the kind of attitude that is adopted by only a few people in the industry. That doesn't mean though it is any less effective. If you're giving advice about a matter that you're not completely certain about and decide to back your opinion with very complicated-looking charts that are based on analyses that seem equally complicated, then you will end up with a presentation that no one will be able to follow. All so that you can give your presentation some added credibility, even when, deep down, you know that it won't hold up to scrutiny. Given that another ROT you should keep in mind, if you don't want to be a fraud or a charlatan is:

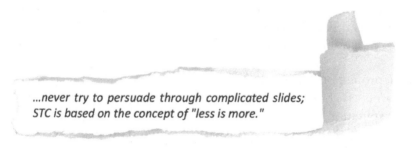

...never try to persuade through complicated slides; STC is based on the concept of "less is more."

Cognitive Ease and the Advantages of Simplicity

Kahnemann defines cognitive ease as the range between what's easy and what is strained (Kahneman, 2011). When something is easy, that means that it's going well, that there are no threats, major news, and no need to redirect anyone's attention anywhere and put in any added effort. When something is strained, on the other hand, then that means there is a problem at hand, which requires that you engage System 2 immediately.

So, why is this important in the context of STC? The reason for this is that when you're presenting or writing a story deck, you need to know when to trigger "easy" and when to trigger "strained." Typically, you should only trigger strained under very specific conditions, like when you want to simulate your audience's memory and retention capability. Otherwise, you should take care to trigger "easy" because when you're dealing with the business world, your brain becomes strained automatically and by default. Your brain is already working hard to keep itself in "easy" mode. So, why would you want to add to that strain?

The way to avoid adding to the strain and keep it "easy" is to make your charts as simple as possible. This doesn't mean making your charts too simple that they become meaningless though. There is an important distinction and Kahnemann explains this concept as follows:

If a sentence is presented in a clear, legible font or it has been primed, then the brain will be able to process it with ease. If, on the other hand, you strain your eyes and brain to read some instructions that have been written using a poor font, faint colors, or if that sentence has been worded in a hard to understand way? Then your brain will strain to process it.

According to experts, the things that trigger cognitive ease include repeated good experiences, good moods, priming, and clear, digestible content. Providing audiences with a presentation that triggers cognitive ease will make them feel content and allow them to feel that what you're talking about is true, familiar, and good. It will also enable them to consume the content you're providing them with effortlessly. In his book, *Thinking Fast, and Slow,* Daniel Kahneman defines cognitive ease as how easy it is for the brain to comprehend a piece of information when it is provided to them. Making things tangible and serving information to the brain aren't endeavors that require a lot of mental energy. Neither does consuming them. We, as human beings, welcome any opportunity to keep things speedy and simple so that we do not waste any cognitive energy.

There is one idiom out there that actually makes this very concept clear: to pay attention. What does asking someone to pay attention mean? It means asking them to "spend" something. When making a presentation the thing you're asking your audience to spend is their brain energy. Human beings are notoriously bad at controlling their attention. This is due to the primal brain, which is the guardian controlling how much brain energy we spend and on what.

Before you can even think of selling anything, you must first sell the value of that thing to your audience's energy so that they can process your message. Think about it like this: when was the last time you attended a workshop and thought, "I wish this were harder on my brain" Never happened right? Of course not. Now think back to your childhood. Your favorite teachers were probably those that made learning an easy and fun experience.

This same kind of logic applies to persuasive messages. An audience you're trying to persuade isn't prepared to hear or read all the different explanations you have on hand for them. So, you have to take the burden of making your message as short, crisp, and simple as you possibly can. That way it will take them mere seconds to grasp that what you're offering them is the best decision they can make.

There is no audience in the world that would ever complain that your message was too easy to understand. On the contrary, most people will stop paying attention to your message if they find it too abstract.

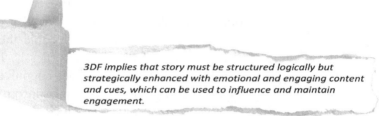

3DF implies that story must be structured logically but strategically enhanced with emotional and engaging content and cues, which can be used to influence and maintain engagement.

If you're trying to sell something like a physical product, then, you have to get the attention of your audience's primal brain. This is because the product in question has a physical, concrete form. If you're trying to sell something like a software or financial service, then you face a much bigger challenge, which is to make that product tangible. Meeting this challenge is important though, because whether something is easy or difficult to understand plays a direct part in your audience's decision-making process. Cognitive neuroscientists and psychologists refer to this as either cognitive fluency or processing fluency (Unkelbach, 2006). The easier something is to understand, the more likely someone will be to decide on it. The harder something is to understand, the less likely they'll be to decide on it. It's as simple as that.

To recap, so far we have talked about the two operating systems of the brain, known as System 1 and System 2, which Daniel Kahneman explores in his book *Thinking Fast and Slow*. System 2 is the lazy part of the brain, the one that people don't like using. We have also discussed the left brain, which deals with logic, and the right brain, which deals with emotions and engagement. You have to get all of these things to work together in STC to convince your audience of the story that you're telling. This can be done through narrative.

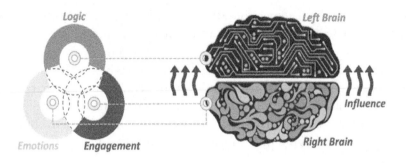

Translating a Main Argument Into a Compelling Narrative

A key aspect of storytelling with charts is translating your presentation's main argument into a compelling narrative. Imagine that you're facing a jury. You have a case to make but the proof you have is ephemeral. This means that said proof appeals to the jury's emotions and may involve manipulation of the mind. You might think that this means you can't get your case to stand but you would be wrong. In a lot of cases, aries can vote for or against something based on how convincing or skilled a lawyer or prosecutor is, even if their evidence isn't rock solid (Lambert, 2022).

To get a jury or your audience to believe in the case that you're making you have to tell a good story. A good story uses both empirical narrative techniques and logical proof. In other words, it combines logic with persuasion strategies. To achieve this, at least three of the following dimensions need to align in your presentation and story:

- Relating to a story (case study).
- The promise of a big idea (emotion).
- Hope (emotion).
- Proof (logic).
- Tension increased through curiosity (emotion).
- Intellectual interest (logic).

The Anatomy of STC-Based Presentation

As mentioned previously, whatever story you're telling in a presentation, your overall goal is to ask something of your audience. The ROT of doing so is to use 20% of the message you're giving to ask your audience to take action. The remaining 80% of your message should focus on content that will automatically lead them to take the action you want them to take. Alternatively, it can focus on getting them to look forward to hearing what you would be asking them to do when you're done with your presentation. This structure can be compared to that of an orchestra which builds up the crescendo of a movement by adding one instrument at a time to it. This is exactly what you want to do until the messages you're giving pile on top of one another, making up 80% of your content.

You should only ask your audience for something once you have completed the story and thus reached its climax. Your goal here is to leave them wanting more and then to deliver your pitch.

This is the correct point to deliver your pitch because by now your story will have allowed you to build trust with your audience. It will also have helped you to build anticipation, so much so that you no longer have to convince them of your pitch. As an example, let's say that you're pitching to an investor. In this case, you'd spend 80% of your presentation building your case with 3DF. Then you'd dedicate the remaining 20% to your pitch and explaining your deal.

As an example, if you're pitching an investor, you'd spend at least the first 80% building your case with the 3DF, and dedicate no more than the last 20%, at the most, to pitching and explaining the deal.

In the following chapters, you'll learn what constitutes a message and a story. But before we get into those details, let's define the following terms as they are the two main dimensions that make up the anatomy of an STC-based presentation.

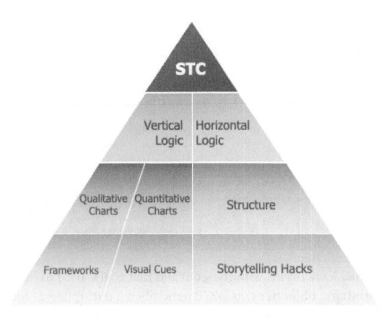

ROT: Think of the story as a series of individual messages that add up to a full story. If we go back to the language analogy, we can think of the messages as the vertical logic. You can think of the words, sentences, and expressions as the horizontal logic that puts them in a sequence that you then use to express yourself.

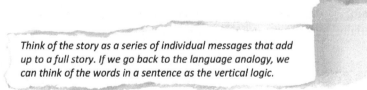

Think of the story as a series of individual messages that add up to a full story. If we go back to the language analogy, we can think of the words in a sentence as the vertical logic.

Horizontal Logic

A story is typically made up of what are commonly referred to as horizontal logic and vertical logic. Horizontal logic is alternatively called the horizontal flow or flow of the story. How a narrative flows is your starting point when structuring a story or at least it should be.

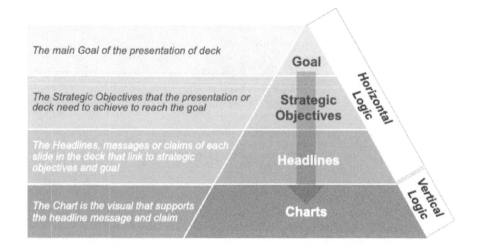

Horizontal logic begins with the **goal** and that goal is used to determine your **strategic objectives,** as you'll remember. Your strategic objectives can be further split into main messages, which can in turn be broken down into individual headlines. These **headlines** can then be supported in **charts**, which are then put into a full story deck.

Though these terms will be further elaborated on when we're covering the STC framework, it's important to keep this pyramid in mind when you're working on the flow of a story.

Horizontal logic, as you'll discover later, is the fundamental structure of your storyline and how you can improve it with storytelling hacks, which will, again, be discussed later. Your story deck, meanwhile, is how you substantially enhance your story, using storytelling hacks.

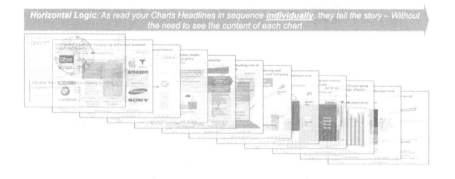

Horizontal logic has several moving parts and has both artistic and creative aspects to it. In contrast, vertical logic is more straightforward, in that it follows a system or a process to reach a conclusion.

Vertical Logic

A chart is the individual slides that make up a presentation. These are also known as vertical logic. Vertical logic can often be mistakenly seen as an art, but in reality, there's a great deal more science to it than that. What's more, it can be more easily mastered through a structured approach and system that, when followed, can be very effective. That doesn't mean, however, that you can't be creative when working on vertical logic. You can, as you will see later on, in detail. This means that you do not have to sacrifice creativity for science and can retain both within the confines of vertical logic.

An individual chart is known simply as a "visual" element. Such elements are designed to back given messages, which are usually written at the very top of charts. These header messages have a variety of names, such as the "lead in," "action title" and "caption." As you'll see later, vertical logic charts consist of qualitative charts containing frameworks, conceptual charts, and quantitative charts, which can be enhanced using visual cues.

An ROT to remember about charts is that you should follow the One Message Per Chart Rule. This is the one rule to rule all rules about charts. Put simply, this means that a single chart shouldn't support more than one key insight made in a presentation.

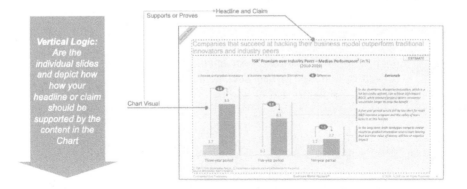

Another ROT is to give one message per slide. Presenting two things on two different slides takes the exact same amount of time that presenting two things on one single slide takes anyways.

Always try to stick to the "One Message Per slide" Rule

Repurposing Horizontal Documents

Horizontal documents, not to be confused with horizontal logic, are documents that make up individual slides designed in landscape format. These, therefore, flow horizontally, from slide to slide. Thanks to modern software tools, current presentations can jump from slide to slide and zoom in and out although there is always a flow that is designed to be a sequenced slideshow.

Horizontal documents are, understandably, the focus of this book. These documents tell single stories and give individual messages on individual slides. They can, however, easily be repurposed and converted into vertical documents and videos, so long as there is a structure in place. Once you have finalized your structure, you can extract whatever you'd like from your horizontal documents and reformat them.

Given that, another ROT is to always start with horizontal documents and then convert to videos or vertical documents later.

Always start with horizontal documents and then convert to videos or vertical documents later.

Converting to Videos

If you build a horizontal document using popular softwares like PowerPoint or Keynote, then you will be able to convert your slides into videos without any issues. You'll be able to add animations to your slides, for example. You'll also be able to animate boxes and charts, so that they do things like appear, disappear, and move. You'll even be able to make them interactive. Additionally, you'll gain the ability to add video rushes and clips between slides. Personally, I prefer recording the narrative and then sending the presentation I've made to my videographer who can then turn it into a video within 24 hours.

Converting to Vertical Documents

A vertical document, not to be confused with vertical logic, is a document or report that follows the structure of a horizontal format, similar to the one in this book. The narrative of vertical documents is supported with charts and visuals but its main flow is designed as text. You can convert a horizontal document into a vertical one by expanding your narrative and explaining the charts found on every slide using words. To accomplish this, I usually run through my presentation as if I were actively presenting it to an audience and record myself. Then I have the recording transcribed by an assistant and voila! Now, I can move from a transcription to a full report by simply editing said transcription. You can too by simply stripping out the main message and using the chart you have as graphs that support the vertical narrative.

Acronyms

As you have no doubt noticed, I use a variety of acronyms in this book that are specific to me. These acronyms are to help you retain important concepts, hacks, tips, and tricks once you have finished reading *Storytelling With Charts*. To keep you from getting lost in these acronyms though, here is a full and easy-to-look-up table. I hope you won't have to refer to it too often but you always can if you need to:

Acronym	Description
3DF	Three Dimensional Framework (logic, engagement, emotions)
Acronym	Spell-Out
ROT	Rule of Thumb
STC	Storytelling With Charts
TA	Take Action
TUG	Two Universal Goals
TBI	The Big Idea
5is	The Five Ideas
AND	Analytics, Narrative, Dopamine
HL	Horizontal Logic
VL	Vertical lOGİC
5SUF	5-Step Universal Framework
TVMA	Time, Number of Variables, Message Attribute

Recap

- The brain has two processes of thinking: one logical and the other emotional. These processes are known as System 1 and 2 and they both should be used in presentations to engage audiences and keep them engaged.
- It's more important to establish your presentation's goal and strategic objectives than to waste too much time trying to understand your audience.
- Your strategic objectives are the main purposes of the story you're telling.
- If you want to convince your audience of an idea or get them to take action on something, you need to speak to both sides and systems of their brain. In other words, it should target both the emotions and logic.
- Emotions and framing play an important part in the decision-making process. As such, your presentation needs to make use of emotions and use emotional triggers.

- You must avoid mistakes at all costs, as making even a single one can cause your presentation to be completely discredited and disbelieved.

- You shouldn't make overly complex-looking charts and slides to appear intellectual as this will backfire. Use charts and slides that are simple but not too simple instead.

- Aim for cognitive ease rather than strain at all times and make sure that everything in your presentation is instantly understandable and easy to grasp.

- STC is made up of both vertical logic (charts) and horizontal logic (storytelling) which essentially work together.

- Your goal throughout the presentation is to evoke interest and curiosity, make your audience want more, and then deliver your pitch at the very end, in response to those emotions.

- Think of the story as a series of individual messages that add up to a full story. You can think of the words, sentences, and expressions as the horizontal logic that puts them in a sequence that you then use to express yourself.

- Start with your story's goal, then your strategic objectives. Then move on to your headlines and finish with your charts.

- Always stick with the "one message per slide and chart" rule.

Chapter 2: Tuning STC to How the Mind Works

Truth is the function of the beliefs that start and terminate among them. –William James, American philosopher and the founder of psychology education

I was scrolling through Netflix the other day, when I came across a documentary about flat-earthers called Behind the Curve. I quickly skimmed over the description but didn't realize that it was a real-life documentary. So, I was expecting a comedy when I first started watching, then I thought maybe it was a spoof documentary. The documentary focused on a community of people based in the US. Some of the members of this community were engineers and other such educated people. Regardless of background, they all believed in the same conspiracy theory about how the earth was actually flat. So, they called themselves the flat-earthers. How on earth could all of these educated people come to believe in such a thing?

I am using this example here to show that there are people out there who hold onto strong, though sometimes erroneous beliefs for a variety of reasons. They hold tight to these beliefs, even when there's clear evidence at hand showing that they're wrong, like the flat-earthers. Chris Argyris, the Harvard professor who invented a concept known as the Ladder of Inference, suggests that something called self-sealing logic through defensive reasoning is responsible for this.

Self-sealing logic is the kind of logic that we form around our beliefs. This logic makes us find information that confirms whatever we believe in and ignores the evidence and truths that could object to or challenge our belief. Put simply, we settle on one belief, which Argyris dubbed our governing beliefs, and seal it off from additional outside information. When someone tries to introduce outside information that can refute that belief, we get defensive and refuse to listen (Riebel, 1996).

Why does this matter in the context of STC? Well, let's say you are giving a presentation to a room full of people and one audience member happens to believe in the exact opposite of what you're making a presentation on. If this is the case, then you are going to have a tough time making your case to that person because they will keep poking holes in your arguments and claims. They'll keep asking you for more proof and no amount of it will be enough or effective. So, you'll be unable to change their mind no matter what you do.

Trying to convince your most skeptical audience member of what you're saying will be like trying to convince a flat-earther that the earth is actually round. However, building a story so that it can be convincing enough to get even that skeptical person on board is a good idea. After all, if you can convince the most skeptical person in the audience of what you're saying, then you'll be able to convince everyone else of it too. In fact, doing so will become much easier for you, when you think about it.

This is why it's important to have someone challenge every claim you make in a presentation. When you're working on a presentation, you can recruit a friend or a colleague to be that person. That way, you can spot any holes in your arguments, cover them and come up with the evidence you need to bolster them, before you have to give your presentation. If you don't have anyone that can serve as your skeptical audience member, then what you can do is step away from your story for a day or two and then review it with a critical eye. In other words, you should always assume the extreme as if every claim you make is going to be challenged in the same way a Flatearther would challenge you when you stated that the earth is round.

Though this book isn't about critical thinking and logic, it's important that you familiarize yourself with the fundamentals of both these things. Doing so can keep you from falling prey to fallacies, spot errors, and cover holes in your logic that you might have overlooked otherwise. Failing at reasoning in even a single chart and the claim that it's associated with is something that can discredit you and your entire story.

Logic and Reasoning

When we say "reasoning," we are referring to the philosophy of logic that dates back to early 1300 BC China and the Ancient Greece of 4th century BC, where Aristotle first laid down its foundations. The word logic is derived from the Greek word "logo," meaning sentence. Logic is the set of rules that governs and drives our reasoning abilities and makes thinking in a structured and effective enough manner to solve problems possible. Human beings' very intelligence is often attributed to their ability to reason and solve problems, which is why logic and reasoning are at the very core of STC.

There are two kinds of reasoning: inductive reasoning and deductive reasoning. Inductive reasoning relies on patterns and can be used, for instance, to prove a hypothesis. Deductive reasoning relies on rules that can be used to arrive at various conclusions when proving a hypothesis.

One of the things we care most about in STC is whether or not the proofs we provide are able to back the claim we make. We test whether or not it can, using our logic. More specifically, we use horizontal logic, which is a series of claims and arguments that enable us to make a case.

With all that in mind, how can we develop the right approach and avoid potential pitfalls when providing good arguments for the hypotheses and claims we're making during STC? Let's go back to the courtroom example and imagine a prosecutor. A prosecutor's job is to prove that someone is guilty of a crime. To do this, they have to gather as much evidence as they can, so that they can eliminate any reasonable doubt that their audience—the jury—might have. If that prosecutor makes mistakes while making their argument or commits errors of logic, they will end up casting reasonable doubt on their very argument and thus discredit their own case. A fantastic example of this is the glove that didn't fit from the OJ Simpson murder trial. While this trial will be shared as an illustrative anecdote later on, you probably know that the prosecutor introduced a blood glove as evidence on the trial's very first. Sure that the glove would fit OJ's hand, he had the man try it on, in front of everyone and in full view of the cameras. Unfortunately, the glove didn't fit. Thus, it ended up pointing toward the exact opposite of what the prosecutor wanted to imply: that OJ was innocent.

The same logic applies to STC, where a single wrong chart can discredit the story you're telling. It doesn't matter if 99.9% of your presentation is accurate and solid. If so much as 0.1% of it is wrong, you will end up undermining both your presentation and all your hard work. To ensure that this doesn't happen you have to firmly understand how logic and reasoning work and how you can use them to their full effect.

Deductive Reasoning

Deductive reasoning is based on simple logic and can lead to definite conclusions based on generally recognized principles. It usually begins with a more general statement and leads to a conclusion. It's a methodology that is adopted by mathematicians and scientists the world over, when they're trying to prove their own hypotheses.

To better understand how deductive reasoning works, let's look at a quick example of it:

1. Companies that either operate in competitive markets or are in the business of selling commodity products are not monopolies.
2. ACME Inc. operates in the competitive market.
3. Therefore, ACME is a NOT monopoly.

As can be seen from this line of logic, the conclusion that is reached is that ACME isn't a monopoly. The starting point of this argument is a definition of "non-monopolies" and this definition assigns specific attributes to companies that operate in competitive markets. The following statement—statement #2—demonstrates that ACME belongs in the world of non–monopolies. Statement #3 arrives at the conclusion that it does using the two bits of information that earlier statements had concretely provided.

As you can see from this example, deductive reasoning is a method that works from the top down. Its main drive is general premises/statements which are used to arrive at logical conclusions that prove your hypothesis, so long as those initial premises are true.

Of course, using deductive reasoning is much harder to do (and sometimes proves an impossible task) in the business world. It's also a more painstaking process in the business world, as proving claims can take much longer than anticipated. At the same, deductive reasoning can be utilized to disprove a given hypothesis. Going back to the above example, one can use deductive reasoning to conclude that the statement that ACME is not a monopoly cannot be upheld. Deductive reasoning can be used to indicate this by bringing in the example of a company known as Luxottica Group.

Luxottica Group is a retail company that designs, manufactures, and distributes eyewear and controls over 80% of the designer brand eyewear on the market. It's considered by many to be a monopoly in this niche, which therefore casts doubt on the statement that companies selling commodity products can't be monopolies. Eyewear can be considered a commodity product yet Luxottica Group is considered by many to be a monopoly. If the Luxottica Group can be considered a monopoly and produces commodity products, then the statement that companies making commodity products aren't monopolies is incorrect. Hence, the statement that ACME isn't a monopoly can also be considered incorrect.

As you can see from this example, the conclusions you arrive at using your deductive reasoning skills are only as strong as your initial arguments are valid. If a generalization that you start with is a weak one or has holes in it, then the conclusions you arrive at using deductive reasoning will be similarly weak or full of holes.

Inductive Reasoning

What about inductive reasoning then? In my experience, you'll find that logic, when adopted in an atypical, STC-based deck, follows inductive reasoning methods. This is because proving claims by making solid, general, and absolute statements is a painstakingly lengthy, boring, and difficult undertaking. Inductive reasoning works from the bottom up. The inferences it makes come from a probabilistic method that is quite powerful, though it does have its own limitations.

Let's say that you're trying to prove the statement that "ACME's cost is too high" which is something you've been told by executives during interviews. This is a general statement that needs to be expanded on and scoped out, before you proceed with gathering evidence that can support it. To do that, you'll need to ask various questions, such as:

- What does "high" mean specifically? For example, is it relative to ACME's competitors? Is it in comparison to the previous year?
- What is the cost referring to? Does it denote product cost, staff cost, or something else?

By asking questions like these, you can turn general statements into more specific and sample-based statements. These specific statements are used and relied on more in the STC and the business world overall than other kinds.

Now, let's say that we are trying to prove that "ACME's direct product cost is too high relative to its competition" using inductive reasoning. To achieve this, we would need to compare cost components like direct labor and materials used in products of ACME and its competitors, assuming that this information is readily available, of course. If ACME has hundreds of competitors, we won't be able to make comparisons between it and all these other companies. What we will have to do is compare ACME's cost to that of its top 10 biggest competitors. If we discover that the cost of ACME's competitors is 20% higher than ACEM's, then we'll have to revise our original statement and say, "ACME's direct product cost is 20% higher relative to the market's top 10 leaders."

As you can see from this example, inductive reasoning will allow us to get very specific in both our hypothesis and reasoning. What's more, when we use inductive reasoning we don't need the data of the entire universe of competitors we're making comparisons with to be able to make sound claims.

The key thing to consider about using reasoning in STC isn't which kind of reasoning skills you should use but how to adopt those reasoning skills in STC. In STC, you can consider inductive reasoning a method that can direct the mind to connect the dots between multiple facts, ideas, and occurrences within a specific context. It can do so by getting the mind to notice similarities and then interpret and articulate them in a way that makes drawing conclusions backing a claim or hypothesis that is being made.

The challenge of inductive reasoning is that it requires some creativity. This is especially true where problem-solving is concerned and let's face it, problem-solving is required in pretty much everything. Whatever goal or objective you've adopted in a presentation, you can view it as a problem that you're trying to solve. You can even say that you're in the business of problem-solving when you're working on strategic issues. To be able to solve problems, you need to make sure that your reasoning is sound. You also need to ascertain that inductive reasoning is something that comes intuitive to you. If it isn't, then that means you need to practice your intuitive reasoning skills within the STC framework, which you'll come to master once you've finished this book.

Issues, Problems, Problem-Solving, and Strategy Applications

As important as your reasoning skills are, you shouldn't waste your time or energy on trying to distinguish between inductive and deductive reasoning and whether you should use one or the other. What you should be focusing on is to ensure that you're using sound logic, regardless of what kind of reasoning you've utilized in coming up with your proof.

One way to accomplish this is to think of developing an STC–based presentation or deck as a problem that you're trying to solve. An ROT to abide by in this regard is to follow the logic of your problem-solving skills to structure and draft an effective presentation, thereby solving your "problem."

Follow the logic of your problem-solving skills to structure and draft an effective presentation, thereby solving your "problem."

Presentations and decks are almost always like solving problems, whether your audience is aware of the problem or not. Whatever conclusion, solution, or recommendation you arrive at the end of your presentation, you can always frame it as a problem. You can then follow the logic of problem-solving. In the coming chapters, we'll dive deeper into a structured framework on how to do that, but for now, all you need to know is how you can convert everything into a "**Universal**" problem and issue a context that will govern your STC.

If you are introducing new findings to the world that go against conventional wisdom or knowledge, your "issue" is that conventional wisdom is wrong. Your "Problem" is to build a case showing why conventional wisdom is wrong. To do this, you need to show that your new findings are correct and so ensure that you have unquestionable proof to back them. As an example, if you were Galileo Galilei, your issue would be that the belief "the sun revolves around the world" is wrong. Your claim would be that the world revolves around the sun and your problem would be proving that claim, thereby going against widespread belief.

As another case example, let's say your business, ACME Inc., is doing very well organically but you are looking for a way to grow sales beyond how they have been organically expanding so far. To do that you need to come up with a strategy. Your main "issue," then, is figuring out which strategy to adopt and your problem is what you should do to grow sales.

If you are developing a strategy to do this, you need to frame and examine it in a story. To tell a story in the STC format, you first need to establish what your context and goals are. In this example, your goal is for the business in question to grow its sales above and beyond their current organic growth level. Once you've identified your goal, you can move on to framing your strategic objectives. This will allow you to identify concrete, optimal, and feasible strategies to grow sales in a way that would add substantial value to the company, without straining its current resources.

The way to go about doing all this is illustrated in the framework below. For now, don't focus on how to come up with a framework—that will be covered in detail later. Instead, focus solely on your options to grow market sales, which, in this framework, have been divided into two main categories, as you can see. These categories are scale, scope, and the options that fall into these categories have been illustrated in a simple 2x2 matrix. This matrix divides those options into new and existing product strategies horizontally and new and existing market strategies vertically:

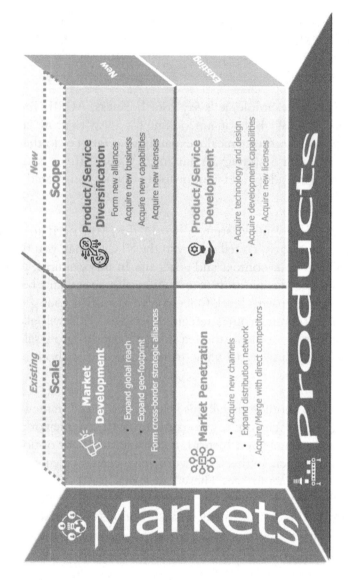

In light of this, we can now frame the issue at hand by asking the following question: Given these strategic options, what is the optimal course of action (i.e. strategy)—which could consist of one or multiple options—for ACME Inc. to adopt to grow its sales? Can ACME adopt at least one of these options or should it stay away from them altogether?

Now that we have this framework in place, structuring the problem logic becomes much easier. Of course, creativity still has a part to play in this, as there are many ways of structuring that problem. For the purposes of this example, let's say that one sub-issue is deciding what the guiding principles we need to use when selecting or rating the given options. Another sub-issue is figuring out how each of these options rank against these criteria: A further sub-issue might be what the pros and cons of the winning options would be if ACME proceeded with them.

Now that we have gotten all that out of the way, let's finally take a look at a problem–solution business case. Say that the CEO of ACME Inc. believes that ACME's cost is increasing. Your goal is to ascertain how this increase started happening and which costs are increasing specifically, then devise a strategic plan to fix the issue. In the above example, assuming ACME is doing well in terms of sales growth, the available options include not changing anything at all and maintaining the current course, a la "if it ain't broke, don't fix it." When it comes to problem-solving, though, things might go a little differently. If you don't tackle an existing problem, then it can get much worse over time. This is why you'll need a course of action, meaning a way to change something.

In problem–solution cases, a good starting point is to split the problem and solutions into main issues and write down the additional sub-issues each one has. In this case, your main "issue" is "Is product cost increasing (Issue 1) and if it is, what should be done to fix it (Issue 2)?"

To draft your presentation you need to identify what the "problems" that are responsible for the cost increase are. That way, you can recommend a course of action at the end of your presentation. Identifying problems in this way is what's known as root cause identification. Assuming that we're talking about direct product cost increases, one of the sub-issue of the case is "What is the direct cost breakdown?" Another is "How has the product cost (by direct sub-cost category) changed in the past years in absolute terms and percentage of sales?" A last one would be "What are the direct and root causes of the cost increase?"

Now that the problem has been structured logically and the root causes have been identified, the next step has to do with the second main issue, which requires that we come up with possible recommendations to fix the problem at hand. These recommendations must tackle the root causes of the problem, if they are to succeed. This can be done for every layer of root causes (as some are short-term while others are structural and long-term solutions). We will get into the detailed methodology on how to accomplish this later on in this book.

Reasoning and logic subjects are usually taught in high school logic courses. As such, they should be familiar, if not second nature to most people. However, sometimes even the most logical of thinkers can fall for the most trivial cognitive biases and commit errors of logic. As such, it's a good idea to go over biases in logic and reasoning skills and take a look at how they affect STC. For those who want to explore the matter further, however, taking a look at Daniel Kahneman's Thinking Fast and Slow would be a good bet.

A good trick you can try to practice your logic skills and avoid committing errors in logic is to try and solve a quick puzzle like the ball problem:

A ball and a bat cost $1.10. The ball is actually $1 cheaper than the bat. If that is the case, how much does the ball cost by itself?

3DF Deep Dive: The Mechanism With 3DF

Having covered the fundamentals of logic and reasoning, let's now take a closer look at the Three Dimensional Framework or 3DF. In the previous chapter, we had likened 3DF to a combustion engine and said that three components worked together to keep this engine running. These components were logic, emotion, and engagement. The main purpose of 3DF is to influence your audience and ultimately persuade them to take action (TA). But what does TA mean specifically? How do the mechanics of getting your audience to take action work?

Before answering those questions and exploring this subject on a deeper level, let's quickly recap: As Kahneman explains, your brain has two systems known as System 1 and System 2 which interact with each other in dual processing. System 1 operates automatically and System 2 operates in a relaxed, low-effort state using only a small portion of its overall capacity. System 1 continually generates impressions, intuitions, goals, and sensations for System 2. When supported by System 2, these impressions and intuitions turn into beliefs and impulses, which in turn transform into deliberate acts. When everything goes smoothly, which more often than not it does, System 2 adopts the recommendations that System 1 gives, without changing them all that much. Given this, it's usually alright for you to trust your feelings and follow your desires.

System 1 calls on System 2 for support during more precise and specialized processing, which it will need to do when it encounters difficulties in resolving an issue. In other words, System 2 is called into action when System 1 is unable to provide an answer to a given question. When you encounter a problem and experience surprise as a result of this, you experience surprise. This feeling effectively triggers System 2 and makes it take action. Surprise, then, stimulates your attention. After all, System 2 is responsible for your efforts to maintain your composure during this process, especially if you have a sudden emotion like a surprise.

There are two key takeaways you can make from all this. The first is that most of what you attribute to System 2 actually comes from System 1. When things take a challenging turn, however, this situation reverses, meaning that System 2 takes control and has the final say. The way System 1 and System 2 divide labor between the two of them is a very effective and efficient process because it reduces the amount of effort you spend on a given task while improving your performance in the execution of that task. However, System 1 is also prone to committing systematic errors under certain conditions and holds certain biases. It's also unable to switch itself off. This is what happens when, for instance, a word written in a language you know is displayed on a screen. If that screen is in your line of sight, you won't be able to switch System 1 off. You therefore won't be able to keep from reading that word, unless your attention is fully and completely directed elsewhere.

Now that we have gone over how System 1 and 2 work together once more, let's take a closer look at beliefs. More specifically, let's examine what you want your audience to feel during a presentation and what you want them to believe.

When you're making a presentation, you want to make it easy for your audience's brains to understand and absorb your messages. In other words, you want to trigger ease, not strain, in their brains. At the same time though, you don't want to make things too simple and thus trigger those brains' BS detectors. You can accomplish this feat thanks to the three dimensional framework. This is because beliefs lie at the very center of 3DF, allowing you to work them across all three dimensions to ultimately influence your audiences and what they come to believe.

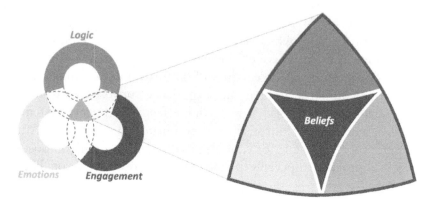

Beliefs

In the previous chapter, I had stressed that not knowing your audience shouldn't be a deal breaker for effective STC. While that is still true, it doesn't mean that you shouldn't understand how your audience's belief system works. Quite the contrary, understanding how beliefs work is vital, as it can give you the ability to influence people's dependency on their belief systems.

Around 20 years ago, people used to believe pretty much anything and everything they heard on the TV, the internet, and other media sources since their exposure to the wider world was more limited. Today, though, that is no longer the case. As the information age has matured, a lot more information has become available to the public. People have all sorts of information at their fingertips, thanks to things like smartphones and AI assistants. At the same time, people are bombarded with conflicting information, fake news, and scam attempts. This situation has caused many to become more weary and reluctant to believe the things that they see and hear. To add insult to injury, now AI is able to create fake content at scale and even impersonate authority figures, spreading misinformation at speeds never possible before in the process. Until such time that the spread of misinformation and fake news can be controlled, people will become increasingly skeptical about any information they encounter and your job as a non-fiction storyteller will become increasingly more challenging.

The information age, then, has birthed a great number of skeptics. This is something you need to keep in mind, seeing a fair number of those skeptics are bound to be among the audiences you make presentations to. No matter what audience you're presenting to, your listeners will most likely be made up of people who believe in different things and have their own understanding of reality.

Take the story of the elephant and the blind men as an illustrative example of this. According to this story, which you're probably familiar with, there once was a king who brought an elephant to his palace. He then invited a number of blind men to his palace as well. The men flocked to the king's side from all corners of the city and the king asked them to touch, feel and smell the elephant, then describe what it is. The sole rule was that the men were only allowed to touch a single part of the elephant.

So, the men gathered around the elephant. One laid his hand on its trunk, the other grasped its tail. One rested his hand on its head, the other on its large body. As a result, the men all came up with different descriptions and interpretations of what they were touching. The first man said that they were touching a snake. The second man, who had hold of the elephant's tale, said that it was a rope. The man whose hand was on the animal's ear concluded that they were holding a large fan.

In the end, none of the blind men could agree on what exactly they were dealing with because they only had access to a single one of its aspects. What's more, they all believed themselves to be right and thought the others were wrong, when in fact they were all wrong. This situation isn't something that's unique to blind men and elephants. Rather it's something that we all go through, as we all see the world and reality just a little bit differently. None of us have access to all of reality. We can only reach aspects of it, bits and pieces, after all. Is it any wonder then, that we all have different beliefs?

In his Incerto book series, which includes Black Swan and Anti-Fragile, among others, author Nassim Talen reiterated that people tend to justify their beliefs by expressing their conclusions first. They then rationalize their conclusions using the proofs that they have selected and ignore the things that might contradict them (Nassim Nicholas Taleb, 2016). This very tendency is why you need to have a goal in mind for your presentations before you start working on them. This goal will be what drives the strategic objectives of the story you're telling. Once you decide on your goal, you'll be able to pick the proofs that will be able to support it.

Previously, we discussed how stories can be solid emotional triggers and how a well-crafted, emotional story can be incredibly persuasive. We have seen how such a story can lower your audience's defensive mechanism and get them to lay down their objections, which they might otherwise have raised when faced with new information. A well-crafted story can take this a step further and influence people's beliefs, even get them to form new ones. In order to understand how this happens, we must first look at how beliefs are formed.

According to Chris Arygris, a belief is formed through single-loop learning and double-loop learning. A single-loop happens when you change your actions after seeing that an outcome you've been expecting as a result of those actions isn't the same as the outcome you have gotten (Argyris, 1977). Typically, you go through single-loop learning, when something goes wrong or something they want to happen doesn't happen. You take this as a sign that you're doing something wrong and adjust your behavior accordingly. Double-loop learning, on the other hand, goes a step beyond that. In double-loop learning something again goes wrong and you become unable to achieve what you're trying to achieve. So, you change your behavior but at the same time, you try to figure out what went wrong, identify the problem, and work to correct it. Double loop learning, then, takes place when you identify the root cause of a problem and come up with a solution for it.

Again according to Arygris, the change in behavior that single-loop and double-loop learning lead to are known as the ladder of influence.

The ladder of inference is something that you should consider when preparing a presentation or finalizing a story deck. It can be adopted as a thinking model to structure your presentation in a way that can influence your audience to take action. To accomplish this, you have to start out with a specific goal in mind. You need to then anticipate all the possible objections your audience might have to your goal. This way you can prepare countermeasures against those objections and find further proof that will lead to your goal. After all, a single counter argument might be enough to kill your persuasion process and cast reasonable doubt on your goal, the same way it would on a point made in a criminal case.

LADDER OF INFERENCE

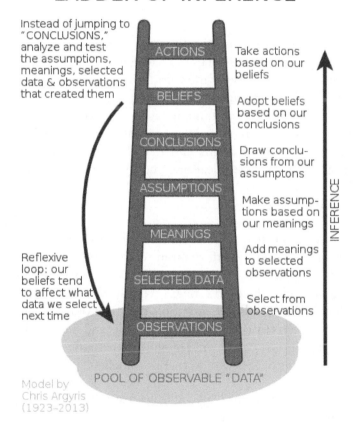

Instead of jumping to "CONCLUSIONS," analyze and test the assumptions, meanings, selected data & observations that created them

Take actions based on our beliefs

ACTIONS

BELIEFS

Adopt beliefs based on our conclusions

CONCLUSIONS

Draw conclusions from our assumptons

ASSUMPTIONS

Make assumptions based on our meanings

MEANINGS

Reflexive loop: our beliefs tend to affect what data we select next time

Add meanings to selected observations

SELECTED DATA

Select from observations

OBSERVATIONS

POOL OF OBSERVABLE "DATA"

INFERENCE

Model by Chris Argyris (1923-2013)

Of course, there may not just be one argument stemming from one belief that will run counter to your argument, belief, and the goal you're trying to accomplish. There may be many such counter arguments and beliefs, all of which can undermine what you're trying to communicate in your presentation. As such, it's important that you anticipate all of these different beliefs and counterarguments and prepare for them, so that by the time you're done none will be left standing. One way to do this is to assess the root cause of a given belief that you are trying to alter. You want to establish why someone might think as they do and believe in certain things. If, for example, you are targeting an organization of sorts, you would be able to establish the root cause you're looking for through investigative research and interviews. Investigative research, on the other hand, is studying the organization you're presenting to by conducting interviews and collecting data that can lead the group of people you will be talking to alter or change their beliefs.

William James has said that "Truth is the function of the beliefs that start and terminate among them" (Thayer, 1977). Our beliefs are our brains' way of making sense of the world we live in and the environment around us. They are mental representations of how our brains expect the reality we live in to be and the things around us to interact with one another. There's an argument to be made that beliefs are ROTs that have been engraved onto our brains and that they have been designed to create shortcuts for efficient learning and decision-making. It can even be argued that beliefs are models of how we can predict the environments around us.

This all makes a great deal of sense since beliefs can help our brains process a large amount of information whenever decisions need to be made quickly, as you will see momentarily. Beliefs save us a lot of time in this regard and reduce how much we rely on the lazy part of our brains. Because of this, beliefs are tools that help our brains to quickly jump to conclusions by connecting various dots and filling in the blanks. Making assumptions based on recognized patterns and incomplete information becomes easier to do thanks to beliefs.

Our brain's default tendency, as you'll again see momentarily, is to take new information and fit it into existing frameworks used to understand the world, rather than having to repeatedly reconstruct that framework every time new information is obtained. It is because of this tendency that we come to take beliefs as true facts. It's because of this that we use these ROTs to navigate our worlds so that we can keep safe. This is the primary reason why we rarely question our beliefs once we have formed them.

A belief, once formed, becomes ingrained in us and turns into something that we take for granted and don't ever question, even if they do happen to be wrong. Our beliefs thus become our subconscious autopilot and give us the ability to tell the difference between things like right and wrong, good and evil, safe and dangerous, true and false, and what's acceptable and what's not.

How Beliefs Are Formed

Beliefs are formed through our experiences, inferences, and deductions. Alternatively, they can be formed through our acceptance of what other people tell us to be true. This is what happens when we are forming most of our core beliefs as children. As newborns, we start the world with a clean slate in that we don't come with our beliefs already uploaded onto our minds. When we're young, our minds are susceptible to the information around us, which we absorb in our attempt to start making sense of the world.

Our biggest source of information tends to be our parents, who play a crucial role in shaping our beliefs. As we start interacting with other children, like our friends, we start influencing one another's beliefs. In this early, developmental stage of our lives, we usually accept everything we are told to be unequivocal truths. Hence there are many kids believing in Santa Clause, for instance. I mean, I know for a fact that it took me a good long while to stop believing in him when I was a kid. For example, this is why many people end up adopting their parents' religions and why belief systems are passed down from one generation to the next.

As the years go by, we start accumulating more and more experiences and these experiences start shaping how we behave. My wife, for example, is ailurophobic—meaning she has a phobia of cats—because she was attacked by a cat when she was a toddler. It has taken her many years and considerable effort as an adult to overcome this ingrained phobia.

Phobias are a good example of deep-rooted beliefs that people can cling to subconsciously, especially since our minds are constantly on the lookout for proofs that could validate them. Most humans, then, think, feel and act based on their beliefs and their past experiences shape how they think, process and interpret new information and form beliefs.

Some time ago, a study was published looking at how we rate various statements to be true. This study found that we have a tendency to think that new details about familiar topics are truer than new details about unfamiliar topics (Begg et al., 1985). In his book, Impossible to Ignore, Carmen Simmons agrees that a human being's entire decision-making process is driven by their past memories and beliefs. If that's true, then motivating audiences to take action is primarily a memory play.

Beliefs and Cognition

The formal education you get in college, the field that you study, and the experience you get from those formative years drive what you think and how you perceive information, along with the environment around you. You can take what happened in the Soviet Union in the 1930s as an example of that.

In the 1930s, the Soviet Union, determined to improve their economy and thus prove that their system worked, went through a bit of a transformation. Till then, people who lived in remote, more urban areas made their living farming and herding animals. Most of them were illiterate, as you may have guessed. But all that began to change in the 30s. Before that change could take place, though a Russian psychologist by the name of Alexander Luria had taken the opportunity to conduct some valuable research. This research had Luria showing skins of various colors to villagers and other rural folk and asking them to group them according to what color they were. That done, Luria then had individuals who lived in more urban areas and were more educated to do the same thing. The results of this simple experiment were truly fascinating because Luria observed that while urban folk could group colors without any issues whatsoever, the rural group could not (Epstein, 2019).

Villages and individuals who had not gotten the benefit of a formal education weren't able to describe the colors of the skins in any formal way. Instead of saying "blue" for instance, they would say things like "the color of the sky." What's more, they weren't really able to see or at least describe the difference between different shades of blue. This difference in perception wasn't just confined to colors though. It was similarly observed in shapes, as well. When villagers were given squares and circles drawn in both broken-up lines and unbroken lines, they were unable to identify what shapes the former were. While they were able to name the shapes drawn with unbroken lines, they didn't call them "squares" or "triangles" or "trapezoids," though. Instead, they referred to them as "the shape of the sun." In other words, they opted to use things they saw as part of their everyday life and the natural world as their reference points (Arunkumar et al., 2021).

The experiment got even more interesting when Luria introduced the Ebbinghaus Illusion into it. The Ebbinghaus Illusion is an optical illusion where an image surrounded by smaller or larger images appears to be smaller or larger than it is (Takao et al., 2019). In his experiments, Luria found that villagers living in remote areas weren't affected by this optical illusion in the same way that educated participants were. The key difference in how the two groups perceived the reality around them was this: the villagers weren't able to see the forest for the trees. The urban group, however, missed the trees for the forest.

The thing is, if you have a certain degree of education, then you have the ability to rely on abstract knowledge. In other words, you have gained the educational experience necessary to solve problems and, if not, to rely on your personal experience. Hence the results that Luria got in his experiments. These experiments very clearly show, then, just how much our experiences shape our beliefs and our cognition, thereby affecting how we perceive and process information.

That said, in face-to-face or in-person encounters, you wouldn't necessarily want to put a conspiracy theorist on the spot and question them about their beliefs. Doing so would backfire for a number of reasons. One reason is that this would end up focusing on a single point of the story in an effort to discredit what they're telling you rather than on the entire story itself. Another is that you cannot know how influential such a conspiracy theorist is in a given audience. As such, you cannot predict how they will impact your narrative. Instead of challenging such dissenters when you're giving a presentation, you should try to listen actively. You should try to engage skeptics to show that they are being heard. You can do this by first establishing a common ground between you and them through a well-articulated, shared vision.

You can then work toward that vision by breaking down the false beliefs and objections that run counter to it one by one.

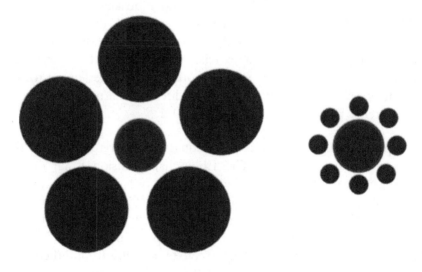

What Do You Want Them to Believe?

When you're working on a presentation, you need to focus on beliefs and potential objections. What they already believe is important but only to an extent. There is no way for you to know what every single audience member believes or how their beliefs might affect their decision-making process, after all. This unknowability is why you should focus on your goal first and then work backward from it to build up a story. Once you have done that, you can build the proofs that will enable you to achieve your goal.

The thing that you want your audience to believe in is the thing that will help them to act and seek the answers that you have to give without putting up any resistance. To get them to believe in that thing, you need to get them motivated to act. You can do this by asking yourself several questions as you start out, like:

- What does the audience need to feel in order to believe?
- What are their potential objections to believing?
- What are their key problems or frustrations?

Analytics, Narrative, and Dopamine

When you're tackling belief, you are expanding on a core aspect of 3DF and doing a deep dive into how to narrate the story you're telling by focusing on analytics, narrative, and dopamine.

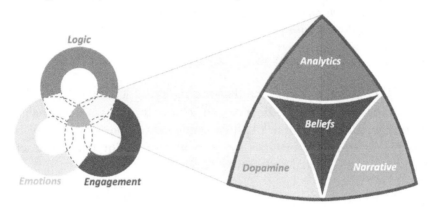

That the 3DF can influence beliefs and motivate audiences to ultimately take action has already been established. The question is "how." The first part of that has to do with analytic and logical reasoning, which will simply be referred to as analytics going forward. Analytic encompasses the analysis work that needs to be done to complete a story deck. It serves two different purposes. The first is to guide your analysis. The second is to tackle beliefs. This latter requires engaging System 2 consistently throughout your story to reassure the logical brain that the story is not all fluff.

Next is the Narrative. The narrative is what brings your analytical story to life. You can have the best story in the world but without a good narrative, it can very easily become a flop. Aside from that, the narrative also influences our beliefs by keeping the user engaged and increasing retention during the process, with the help of visuals, of course. The order in which a narrative unfolds plays an important part in how successful it is.

Without venturing too far into neurology, dopamine is a chemical in the brain which can influence how people take action by boosting the anticipation they feel, along with their expectation of receiving a reward.

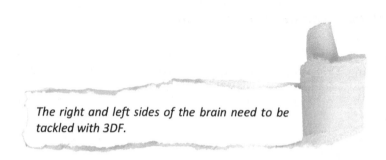

The right and left sides of the brain need to be tackled with 3DF.

One ROT to keep in mind is that the right and left sides of the brain need to be tackled with 3DF. You can achieve this by working Analytics, Narrative, and Dopamine (AND) simultaneously in a story. The best charts and storylines are those that tackle AND simultaneously while driving to the end goal and strategic objectives.

Analytics, Logical Reasoning, and Critical Thinking

Logic is essential for making sure that a story drives to the end goals and strategic objectives you mean to reach. As such, it remains at the core of STC. Developing a story requires using both vertical and horizontal logic. The history of logic can be traced back to the time of ancient philosophers residing in India, China, and Greece. But the logic we're concerned with, within the context of STC, is critical thinking. The Oxford English Dictionary defines critical thinking as "objective analysis and evaluation of an issue in order to form a judgment" (Oxford English Dictionary, n.d.).

Critical thinking is built on logic in both a vertical and horizontal way. Your goal as a presenter isn't to present some fictional idea or scam to your audience. It's to follow a certain kind of logic that is targeting a specific belief. In other words, it's to use a series of logical arguments to get to your goal, otherwise known as your main objective.

Going back to the courtroom analogy, you can think of yourself, the STC presenter, as a prosecutor, and your audience as a jury. The obligation that a person or party has to support their claims or assertions through evidence is known as the burden of proof. In this case, the "burden of proof" lies on you (the prosecutor). Though your audience—the jury—is neutral for the most part, listening to and absorbing everything you're saying, some of its members are firmly planted on the opposite side and thus represent views contrary to your own. The defense attorney representing the other side is one such member. It's these audience members' job to poke holes in your arguments. Despite this, though, your task is to sway your audience and get them to believe what you're saying without reasonable doubt clouding their opinions.

Three kinds of logic apply to this anecdote and are relevant to you: vertical logic, horizontal logic, and the logic of the proof behind the claim you're making in a headline. Seeing as vertical and horizontal logic have already been covered, let's examine various common techniques that can be adopted in the logic of proof.

When you're telling a story, you need to consider that story as being made up of a series of claims. Some of these claims are simply statements and are quite obvious, while others are less so, to varying degrees. A proof, meanwhile, is made up of a sequence of logical statements, which sequentially imply one another. They provide your audience with indisputably, logical, sound explanations as to why a certain claim has to be true.

If you, as a presenter, are unable to prove a specific hypothesis fully and completely, then you need to make sure you phrase your messages in a way that doesn't make them sound like firm statements based on data. Statements not backed proof cannot be presented as absolutes, that is if you want to hold onto your credibility. Your credibility is something that directly impacts how believable the data you're presenting is. This is something that I can confirm through firsthand experience.

Proof and Evidence

To make a case and prove something beyond a reasonable doubt, you need to have the right evidence at hand. This means that you need to have a series of arguments, in this case, your vertical logic, that should be designed in a way that walks your audience through a logical, well-structured journey. This journey can then lead the audience to the emergence of their beliefs, which should line up with your goal.

As an ROT, disproving a claim is typically easier to do than proving it. But if that's the case, how can you ever prove something? You can do so by using the "disprove" principle as much as you can while building your case.

Using the disprove principle means adopting a strategy to disprove the point you're trying to make, while you're trying to make it. In essence, it's poking holes in your own arguments so you can figure out how to fill those holes when your audience tries to do the same. An added benefit of the disprove principle is that it can help you overcome bias by disconfirming evidence, thereby allowing you to pre-empt and exhaust all objections that your proof might be faced with later on.

Proof is a very broad subject within the context of critical thinking and there are many different kinds of proof mechanisms at work. Becoming familiar with the strongest, most common, and most acceptable of these mechanisms is something that can help you a great deal while preparing your presentation.

In consulting, as in most other things in life, the way you build a case using the right kind of proof is an important part of the art of persuasion. This is something that lawyers and prosecutors tend to be very good at. Such people, though, often use evidence-based proof, which, oddly enough, isn't always the strongest proof mechanism you can turn to. This is why sometimes some juries end up passing judgments that do not align with the proof that has been presented in a case. It's also why you can sometimes get a hung jury.

Regardless, becoming familiar with these proof methods and having them ready in your arsenal is still a good idea. This will give you the ability to mix and match different methodologies, depending on how strong your proofs are and how they can function together.

Social Proof and Benchmarking

Seeing the terms social proof and benchmarking together might be a little off-putting. But the reality is that benchmarking is actually a form of social proof. Benchmarking is something that has you compare yourself and the results you get following a performance to your peers and their results. You might alternatively end up comparing yourself to other respectable companies or industry standards or niche standards, for that matter.

Most companies tend to willingly pool their data in a collective unit so that they can compare their performance to that of their competitors. This is how social proof works, isn't it? The very term social proof was invented by Robert Cialdini in his first book, entitled *Influence*, which was published in 1985. As Cialdini explored in *Influence*, most people look at others to determine what the right way to behave is. This is where herd mentality comes from, a phenomenon that influences the behaviors of others in group, community, and societal settings (Shortform, n.d.). The proof that they obtain in these settings is "everyone else is doing this, so it must be right."

Considering this, it can be said that social proof and benchmarking are forms of proof. However, personally, I wouldn't advocate for adopting this type of proof in your line of logic during a presentation. What you could do instead is to very occasionally use it to enhance your claims, as these are strategies that would appeal to most people.

Analogy Proof

Analogy proof is another kind of proof that bears some similarity to social proof and benchmarking. However, unlike them, it draws on single cases or at least smaller groups of cases, as opposed to the large sample sizes that social proofs and benchmarking use. This is the key difference between analogy proof and benchmarking.

Analogy proof looks at a specific case or a small number of cases that occurred under the circumstances that your case is occurring under and learns from the successes and failures that already occurred under those circumstances. The fact that its sample size is smaller than that of benchmarking means that analogy proofs have fewer variables to work with. In benchmarking, you might be looking at different companies of different sizes in different geographies and niches. In analogy, proof would be looking at a singular example from a specific company that matches the parameters of your current circumstances.

Mathematical and Analytical Proof

You've likely come across mathematical and analytical proof methodologies in high school already. To quickly refresh your memory, a mathematical proof is an argument that shows that a stated assumption logically guarantees a given conclusion. At the same time, a mathematical proof uses both inductive and deductive reasoning.

There are two different kinds of mathematical proofs. The first is proof by contradiction. Here, the idea is to write a proposition and then state that it is either true or false. If you have stated that a statement is true, then you go offer proof to the contrary, thereby proving that it is false. If you have stated that it is false, on the other hand, you offer proof that the statement is actually true. In short, you prove or disprove a statement by using contradictions (Malcom, n.d.).

The second kind of mathematical proof is called proof by contrapositive. Proof by contrapositive takes statements like, "If P, then Q" and switches the places of "P" and "Q" to show that while the first statement is true, the second one isn't. An example of this would be "If this is my house, then it is big." Let's assume that this statement is true and then switch its order, thereby turning the sentence into "If this house is big, then it is mine." This statement is patently untrue, seeing it's impossible for the speaker to be the owner of every big house in the world.

Demonstrable or Visual Proof

One last I would like to add is demonstrable or visual proof. This kind of proof simply shows, that is to say, demonstrates, that something works. The problem with demonstrable proof, though, is that it isn't always readily available. If it is available to you, though, it is a powerful method that can demonstrate that a suggested course of action or belief actually works. Alternatively, it can be used to show your audience that something they have been doing or believing is actually not working. If you had a laser and needed to prove that it could cut through steel, for example, then all you would need to do is put on a demonstration showing that laser cuts steel. The demonstration itself would become your visual proof.

Undeniable Facts That Need No Proof—Unquestionable or Obvious Facts

Some statements simply don't need to be proved because they are undeniable facts. That the sun will rise in the morning and set in the evening is an undeniable fact, for instance, unless you live above the Arctic Circle, where some days the sun will not rise for the entirety of the winter. Of course, undeniable facts aren't just found in nature. You can encounter such facts in the data you're working with, as well. If you're going through the inventory count that was just handed to you in a company, for example, then the numbers you're dealing with are undeniable facts, assuming that the data at hand hasn't been forged.

The good thing about undeniable facts is that they cannot be disputed. This means that you don't have to put in any work trying to prove or disprove them, so long as the source you've gotten them from is credible.

Undeniable facts are sometimes also referred to as inspirational proof. The inspirational proof is the kind of proof that appeals to faith. As an example, if you've been to Japan, but have heard of Japan, you would simply have faith that Japan actually exists. You wouldn't require any kind of proof attesting to that fact.

Narrative and the Value of a Good Story

Now that we have gotten a thorough understanding of the different kinds of proof you can use in your story, let's take a closer look at your narrative. In the previous section, we had used a courtroom analogy, where arguments for various cases are made, cases that determine the life of some people. Unlike court cases, you don't need to be in a life-or-death situation to keep people engaged in your narrative. The problem is, though, the cases that you discuss in the business world aren't always all that interesting for everyone in your audience. Given that, framing your cases in an engaging narrative is crucial if you want to keep your audience interested.

A good narrative can be incredibly effective in increasing retention. Obviously, you want your audience to remember your presentation and slides, once you're done presenting to them. As such, you need to be absolutely certain that you have established a good narrative. One way you can test whether you've accomplished this or not is to see if you've been able to get your audience to suspend their disbelief while you're telling your story or making your presentation.

Suspension of disbelief is something that happens when we purposefully disengage System 2 so that we can avoid triggering our critical thinking skills and logic capabilities. We want to avoid engaging these skills because they can be used to overanalyze what's happening in front of us, which would make suspension of disbelief impossible to do. Suspension of disbelief is something you often do when you're reading a fictional novel or watching a movie or TV series. In engaging in these activities, you immerse yourself in the stories they offer and enjoy the reality they depict by believing that they're real.

Since you are unable to tell what different people's beliefs are as you're presenting to them, what you want to do is get them to disconnect from their beliefs. You want your audience to start with a clean slate as you build your story for them, rather than start out with a particular belief. This doesn't require that you try and understand what your audience's beliefs are. Rather it requires that you establish a universal set of beliefs through your story.

The Power of a Good Story

"Why stories?" you might be asking yourself. We need stories because while facts alone may provide us with the information we need, only stories can give people the context they need to connect those facts with different people, situations, and events. In other words, stories give people meaning.

Stories are, essentially, learning tools. Since the dawn of language, stories have been used to convey other people's experiences to others, so that they could learn from them. A good story is a bit like a drug, in that it causes both the storyteller's and the audience's brains to release certain hormones. Brain scans taken of people sharing stories with one another shows that this act actually connects the subjects' brains and makes them mirror one another (McMurray, 2021). Storytelling causes mirror neurons to kick into gear, which is a phenomenon known as neural coupling, as we have seen.

When people reach the stressful, dramatic high points of a story, their brains release a hormone called cortisol. Cortisol is the same hormone that makes your fight–or–flight response kick in when you are under some kind of threat. It also is responsible for your ability to create strong memories of emotional experiences. When the conflicts and difficulties of a story are resolved, on the other hand, your brain releases a hormone called oxytocin. Oxytocin is often released through physical touch and plays a part in your ability to form social bonds with others. It's also responsible for feelings of contentment, calm, and security (Batabyal et al., 2021).

When someone tells you a story, they end up sharing an experience with you and expressing their beliefs about that experience at the same time. While this is going on, your brain couples with your storyteller's brain. In the process, the two of you end up building a relationship of sorts and creating social cohesion. This makes it easier for you to develop shared goals and move toward them.

Given all this, prompting others to tell you stories and listening to them is as much an art as storytelling itself. When you ask someone to tell you a story, you're basically telling them that their experiences matter. You're giving them the message that their opinions have meaning.

The Importance of Narrative

That being said, not all stories are created equal. In order for a story to be effective, it needs to be relatable. If this is accomplished successfully, then that story will short-circuit all cognitive barriers, jump lines drawn in the sand and move directly into a place of trust between you and your audience. From that point of trust, a story can be used to:

- Overcome objections.
- Build on trust.
- Have a eureka moment.
- Provide social proof.
- Create a bond.
- Add interest.

On the flip side, a good story can be thoroughly destroyed if it's not told properly. This is something that I have experienced for myself. I was once at a bar in a lounge in Hong Kong, where something really embarrassing happened to me. A few weeks after this embarrassing but funny incident, I related what had happened to my friend Bill, who was having a cup of coffee with me at the local Starbucks. As I was telling my story to Bill, I noticed that I was having a hard time keeping my friend's attention. Bill simply wasn't able to focus on what I was telling him. Rather than listen to my anecdote, Bill kept getting interrupted by meaningless messages. His constantly beeping phone was of more interest to him than what I was saying.

Needless to say, the story I was telling Bill at that moment didn't prove compelling enough for him to keep focusing on me for more than a few minutes. A couple of weeks after this incident with Bill, I ended up getting dinner with him and two other friends, one of whom, Dan, had been with me in Hong Kong when that embarrassing incident happened. At dinner, Dan launched into his own telling of the same story I had tried to share with Bill. Unlike me, though, he fully captured everyone's attention. His audience neither said a word to interrupt him as he spoke nor kept checking their phone, even though the story went on for a good 10 minutes.

So, what exactly was responsible for this difference? What was so different between my telling of the story and Dan's telling of it? The narrative.

Most people think that the word "narrative" can be used interchangeably with the word "story." But two aren't actually the same thing because the narrative is what brings your story to life and makes it great or alternatively, disastrous. It is therefore what you use to channel your audience's energy directly to your content.

A narrative's job is to define the frame in which a story operates. Given that, a narrative is actually much bigger than a story. It's a whole way of looking at the world and an overarching concept able to influence thought, meaning, and decision-making. Symbolic frames like "The American Dream" or "Just Do It" are actually good examples of narratives, despite how very brief they are. These narratives clearly don't have defined beginnings, middles, and ends the way stories do. However, they still have the ability to unfold over time and offer an ending or conclusion to their audiences, even if they're open-ended ones.

If stories can be considered pearls, then narratives are the necklaces on which those pearls are strung. They are what connect the dots of larger pictures. A good narrative is one that uses a range of stories to illustrate, animate and validate the message that it's trying to give. A narrative can give meaning to a broader vision, provide the audience with a view of what's possible and make clear the reasons why they should head in that direction.

A good narrative, in the context of beliefs, is one that leaves its audience screaming for more, before it goes on to ask them to take action. The action that TV shows like *Lost*, *24*, *Breaking Bad*, and *Game of Thrones* ask their readers to take, for example, is to keep watching or to binge-watch. The narratives of these series drive the momentum forward, leaving their viewers in a state of anticipation from one episode and season to the next. It is this exact feeling that you want to evoke in your audience once you have completed the body of your story, before you move on to asking them for something. The question is, how do you do that, seeing as you're not writing a piece of fiction?

Dopamine, Heuristics, and Cognitive Biases

To evoke the feelings you need to evoke in your audience, you need to play on heuristics and system 2 to steer your listeners' brain chemicals in the direction that will get them to take action. This is something that can primarily be achieved by applying strategies and analytics to stories that make the audience avoid any cognitive biases they may have. It can also be done by using heuristics to steer them toward action, rather than inaction.

According to neuroscientists, dopamine is a hormone that is sent from one part of your brain to another through your neurons, meaning your brain cells. These neurons function together and build an interconnected system, which neuroscientists have dubbed the dopaminergic system (Winn, 2017). The dopaminergic system stretches all the way from the front part of your brain—officially referred to as the frontal cortex—to the mid part of your brain—called the striatum—and a part of your brain, known as the limbic system. The frontal cortex does things like handle your cognitive functions, such as your thinking and short-term memory. The striatum dictates and manages your motor control skills. Meanwhile, the limbic system regulates your emotions and is home to the pleasure and reward center of your mind. When dopamine floods your brain, it makes its way to all three of these sections and thus, plays an important part in motivating you to do certain things. Dopamine, then, is something that can keep you deeply engaged in what you're doing. This means that if you can get your audience's brains to release dopamine while you're making a presentation to them, you can get them to take the actions you want them to take.

The main idea that I'm trying to illustrate using this explanation is that dopamine is inextricably linked to good feelings and positive experiences. This is because such feelings and experiences usually cause people to want or desire something, come to enjoy something, and learn something. Let's say that you have a hankering for ice cream. The craving you feel in that moment is, obviously, the act of wanting. Getting and eating your ice cream is enjoying it and knowing that you will get enjoyment from eating your ice cream is a source of motivation for you.

These three elements essentially work together to motivate you to do something. This "something" might be a pleasurable activity like eating ice cream. But it can also be something like completing a project or assignment, listening to music, reading a book, having a discussion with others... In short, it can be anything and everything that causes your brain to start releasing dopamine.

As briefly mentioned, you want to make your presentation a pleasurable enough experience to get your audiences' brains to start releasing dopamine. In doing so, you want them to be fueled by the pleasant sensations they're feeling and motivated enough to take the course of action you'll be suggesting to them at the end of the presentation. Not only that, but the presentation you're creating should infuse your audience with the sense that they will get the kind of reward they want if they take the action you are suggesting that they take. In other words, you want to get their brains to release dopamine to motivate them to take you up on your idea. You want to create the sense that they will be getting a reward that they really want, by the time they're done listening to you, and prime them to take the actions necessary to go after that reward.

With that in mind, you have to ask yourself what kinds of rewards are motivating enough to get your audience to take action? To answer that question, you need to better understand the factors that get human beings to take action in the first place. You need to remember that staying 100% motivated all the time is impossible no matter who you are and what circumstances surround you. Behavioral science and neuroscience dictate that our motivations are prone to waxing and waning from one moment to the next. As such, behavioral scientists and neuroscientists say that our mood plays a huge part in this (Gullickson, 1996). They also say that how motivated an individual is or not depends on things like their personality traits, how stressed or anxious they are at a given moment, whether or not they've gotten enough sleep at night and rest during the day, whether or not they're hungry, and more. Someone who is distracted by their growling stomach, for instance, isn't likely to be very motivated to finish the project they're working on. At least, not until they've had a sandwich, at the very least.

How can you offer the right rewards and value propositions to your presentations then? To do this, you must get to work on developing an understanding of what an audience considers rewarding. Then you have to work those values and rewards, be they physical, mental, financial, or something else entirely, into your presentation and proposed course of action. You can achieve this by providing your audience with a modicum of uncertainty when communicating the rewards you're offering them. This is an effective strategy because dopamine is known to spike in the face of unexpected events like during surprises. Introducing some ambiguity, then, can be a way of creating such unexpected events and generating some tension among your audience. When creating tension, though, you should keep in mind that people can tolerate a certain amount of tension if they know how much tension they'll be facing. You can create tension in a presentation by providing your audience with some kind of instant gratification, avoiding over-promising by setting expectations and repeatedly reminding your audience of what the final outcome will be. More such hacks to come later!

Don't Fall for the Curse of Knowledge Trap

There's a little observed cognitive bias called the curse of knowledge, sometimes referred to as the curse of expertise. I'm bringing this to your attention because it's something that happens to me all the time. It happens whenever I gain more knowledge and automatically assume that my audience knows the same things that I do, because they have a similar kind of background to my own. This curse is a bit like music. Take for example, a new song that was released and that you listened to several times over the next few days. Now imagine playing this song to others who like the same kind of music as you, assuming that they've been listening to it as well. But then you suddenly realize that they are hearing this song for the first time in their life.

This is how the curse of knowledge trap works. As such, you should never make assumptions about what your audience knows. You should always have backup slides at hand to explain various information, just in case. You can then use these slides whenever you need to further explain or elaborate on something. In the process, you can ensure that none of your audience members are left in the dark.

Biases

I have just finished sitting outside where I was enjoying a cup of espresso at a coffee shop in Florence. I have stood up and am leaning over to tuck my iPad away in my bag, getting ready to leave when some guy running as fast as he can slams into me from behind. My iPad flies into the air, then drops onto the floor, shattering into 1000 pieces... My first thought at that moment is "What an a**hole." But then I look behind me and see what has happened. It turns out that the man was running to attend to his pregnant wife, who had just fainted and collapsed because of the heat. Needless to say, my thoughts about the gut changed instantly, in that very moment. Had I been in his position, I would have reacted in the exact same way.

The reason I'm sharing this story is that it clearly illustrates how our brains work and how our cognitive biases operate. We all have certain cognitive biases whether we realize them or not. Simply knowing that we have them and recognizing them isn't enough for us to overcome our biases. Instead, overcoming our biases can only be achieved by practicing destroying them over and over again and then ethically leveraging them to make our points in STC.

Cognitive biases can actually cause two people looking at the exact same data or charts to arrive at completely different conclusions. Obviously, this is not the outcome you want to achieve when giving a presentation. This is why knowing how to overcome cognitive biases is important. This is something that the authors of the book *Crucial Conversations: Tools for Talking When Stakes Are High* are very aware of, which is why they have illustrated how paradoxically difficult overcoming cognitive biases is.

In *Crucial Conversations*, the authors state that we, as human beings, have been designed incorrectly. As a result of this, we often get into trouble when our conversations turn from routine to crucial. This happens because our emotions don't exactly prepare us in a way that allows us to have an effective conversation. Instead, countless generations of genetic conditioning have shaped humans into beings that handle crucial conversations with their fists, as opposed to intelligent persuasion techniques and gentle attentiveness (Patterson et al., 2012).

One type of crucial conversation where this pattern plays out is a disagreement. Let's say that you are having a disagreement about a subject you care greatly about. Suddenly, you find that the hairs at the back of your neck are standing up. Those you can handle. But at the same time, two tiny organs seated neatly atop your kidneys are pumping adrenaline into your system. This isn't something you've chosen to do. It's something your adrenal glands are programmed to do, something you have to live with.

But that's not all. While all that's going on, your brain starts diverting blood away from every action and reaction that is deemed non–essential to your survival. Things like running or fighting are considered essential by your brain. This means that your larger muscles, like the ones in your legs and arms, start getting more blood. But the higher level reasoning area of your brain? That's suddenly getting a lot less blood. Hence you're having trouble managing this frustrating argument. Hence you're potentially being more willing to respond aggressively and impulsively, rather than logically.

Now let's add another dimension to this. Crucial conversations are seldom planned. Mostly, they occur spontaneously and out of the blue. They catch you by surprise and this results in you having to conduct an extraordinarily complex conversation without being able to properly prepare for it. The only thing you have to work with at this moment is your fight-or-flight instinct. If you've ever found yourself standing on a stage, facing an audience for the first time, this is a feeling you've experienced before. Being nervous on stage or in front of a crowd can easily trigger your fight-or-flight response, making your brain order your heart to divert blood from your brain to your extremities, like your legs, so that you can run. Is it any wonder then that you react poorly during such critical conversations, so much so that you later question how you could have said and done the things that you did?

What all this means is that when we're facing crucial conversations, we often act in self–defeating ways. We act to our detriment rather than to our benefit. In the process, we become our own worst enemies without even realizing it.

The Brain's Operating Systems and Cognitive Ease

Our cognitive biases are born out of decision-making processes that are based on flawed logic and reasoning. This is why seeking the right data to back the claims you'll be making in your presentation while trying to make sense of that data is an essential part of STC, as you'll see later.

As you'll recall, Kahneman has stated there are two systems in our brains: System 1 and System 2. System 1 is the more intuitive of the two and is highly emotional and quick. Given that, it's able to utilize shortcuts known as heuristics. Heuristics are things that allow us to function effectively and rapidly and have been essential to our survival as a species. Heuristics kick in, for instance, when you're being chased by a predator and help you to get away without losing any time on analyzing the threat.

The problem with heuristics is that they can cause your reasoning to become flawed without your realizing it. We already know that we human beings are hardwired to see threats and catastrophes everywhere. This situation is partly responsible for at least some of our cognitive biases. The human brain also prefers ease to strain, as you'll remember. So, it's easier for it to believe System 2 when it goes into effect. Ease depends on repetition, clear display, having a primed idea and even being in a good mood. By this logic, then, if you were to repeat a falsehood enough times and under the right conditions, you could get people to accept it, even if it was untrue. The incorrect concept would thus become easy to accept and so a cognitive bias would be born.

Biases Impact Your Analytical Process

As previously mentioned, biases come into being when the brain takes shortcuts and applies rules of thumb to all sorts of different areas. If this is how you and your audience form cognitive biases, then what are you to do? In this case, you need to counter potentially false "rules of thumb" by adopting carefully selected counter rules and practicing them on an ongoing basis. In doing so, you can make combating cognitive biases second nature to you and make your STC practically bulletproof.

When you're making a presentation in person or sending a report out to others, you might end up getting into a back-and-forth with someone who holds cognitive biases that counter the message you're trying to give. If this back-and-forth takes place in writing, then you'll have plenty of time to think before you act. In an in-person presentation, however, you'll have less time to think logically about your response. In such circumstances, system 2 might try to take hold of your responses and your own cognitive biases might start filtering into them.

Evolutionary psychology suggests that our biases have evolved much in the same way that our hands and feet did. Since cognitive biases can lead to perceptual distortions, and cause us to make inaccurate judgments and illogical interpretations, they are relevant to STC in two ways. The first way is how your own cognitive biases can affect the way you build your case and supply proof for it. These biases can thus cause you to make inferences that you really should avoid making, which will ultimately discredit you and your whole story. The second what how your cognitive biases might affect the flow of your story and the way in which you're trying to influence your audience.

To prevent cognitive biases, which may otherwise affect how you come up with the content you'll use in your presentations, you must become aware of them and the triggers that cause them to kick in. You must also strive to make that effort a regular habit you automatically reach for. When you think about it, all your thoughts can be considered habits of sorts, as the philosopher Charles S. Pierce suggests (Burch, 2014).

Implications

In a famous psychological study, Solomon Asch described two different kinds of people to his audience and asked them to make comments about their personalities. These people were named Alan and Ben. When evaluating Alan and Ben, based on the information that Asch had given about them, the audience said that Alan was intelligent, critical, impulsive, industrious, envious, and stubborn. They also said that Ben was stubborn, intelligent, critical, impulsive, and industrious.

When hearing these descriptions, most people consider Alan a more likable person compared to Ben. This is because Alan is described as stubborn last and Ben is described as stubborn first. Though they are stubborn, the order in which the adjective is used to describe them changes the meaning of the rest of the adjectives that are applied to the two. For instance, stubbornness in an intelligent person is generally considered to be justified. It can even be respected. In contrast, intelligence in a stubborn and envious person causes us to consider them as dangerous. This is what's known as the halo effect.

The sequence in which we observe characteristics and adjectives is determined by chance in most cases. Not so in presentations, where you are telling the narrative and therefore literally have the ability to put your words in any order you'd like. Sequence matters because the halo effect can alter the weight that first impressions carry. It can cause your audience to pay more or less mind to the information you give following the first impression you make.

A great example of this is seen in the story that a university professor had to tell. Early on in his career, this professor used to grade his students one at a time. He'd pick up a test booklet and read all that student's essays one after another. He'd grade them as he went. Then he would calculate the total and move on to the next student. Over time he noticed that the way he evaluated and graded the essays had become strikingly similar to one another. He suspected that the situation might have to do with the halo effect, in that the way he graded the first question disproportionately affected how he graded the subsequent ones. If the student in question got a high mark on the first question, he'd keep getting high marks on the rest. If not, then the reverse would be true.

Understandably, the professor concluded that this situation was unreasonable and maybe even unfair. So, he decided to change the way he graded his students' tests. Instead of reading the booklets in sequence, he first graded all the students on their first question. Then he did the same with the second question, then the third, and so forth. To make sure he wouldn't get biased, he wrote down all the scores on the inside pages of the booklets. In changing up his approach like this he noticed just how much the halo effect had been influencing him.

Having noticed this, the professor also realized that the things he did to get the halo effect under control conformed to something known as the decorrelate error. The decorrelate error happens when, say, a large group of people is given a jar with pennies in it and are asked to guess how many pennies are inside. This is a task that most people would do miserably at. Pools of people though? Not so much, since some people overestimate how many pennies there are and others underestimate it, making them meet in the middle. That middle tends to be accurate or close enough to be accurate anyways. The decorrelate error, then, circumnavigates individual errors people might make.

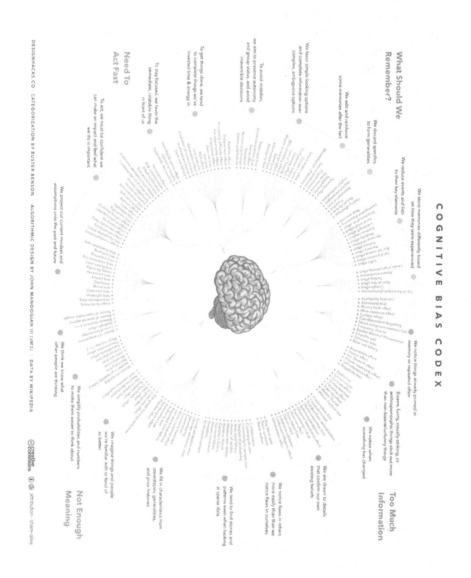

If you're trying to extract the most useful information from multiple different sources to use as your proof in your presentation, then first you need to make sure that your sources are separate and independent. That way, you can make use of the decorrelate error. This is why, for instance, police officers would talk to multiple witnesses at the scene of a crime rather than just one. Considering all this, it can rightly be said that the way we make judgments, word things, and use different sources to decorrelate errors, then, have an immediate impact on our presentations.

Memorable Content and Why It Matters

Creating memorable content is among the most important, yet underutilized techniques of STC. Sometimes even the pros miss its importance. Nonetheless, as you'll discover next, leading strategy consultants deploy some of these techniques in qualitative verticals and the horizontal structure, albeit without realizing the importance of memorization as a strategic objective in STC.

So, why exactly is memorable content important? Let's say you have solid reasoning built into your presentation and that you invested a lot of time in making your case. To do so, you had to go through numerous issues, sub-issues, and hypotheses so that you could arrive at your final conclusion and recommendation. This naturally involves having your audience "take action," as discussed previously. What would happen, if when you reached the end, your audience couldn't remember all the claims you made and proofs you offered, which include beliefs, and the breaking down of all objections?

As you recall, if you fail to tackle a strong belief that runs against your claims, your whole argument can come tumbling down and discredit the presentation. If that's true, wouldn't this alone be grounds to make sure your audience remembers every key content in your presentation? You may be thinking, what if you were to add a recap (summary) at the end of your presentation or pitch, in order to refresh people's memory? This, on the whole, is a good idea. Now, let's assume that your audience managed to recall the entire flow of your presentation and ultimately, believed you by the end of it. Let's also assume that they were willing to "take action." There are two problems in relying on recaps alone to accomplish this. The first is that while a recap may emphasize a claim, you may have a great many chained claims or messages. So, you cannot possibly recall all of them along with what their proof was in just a few minutes. The second problem with recap is how long it would take for a belief to be remembered, and how long the urgency of having to "take action" would last. In such cases, this urgency only lasts a short while, such as an hour, a day or, at maximum, a week. That is if what you presented wasn't vividly memorable at the end, though. After all, most calls to action are typically intended for the long term, as opposed to the moment.

Given all the work you're putting into your presentation, would you want the urgency of what you are presenting to last as long as possible? Wouldn't you at least want it to stick in your audience's mind permanently? If so, then you would want to think about making your content that has a lasting impact and can be engraved in the long-term memory of your audience.

Memorable content is a necessary and must-have ingredient to create persuasion. But on its own, it cannot be used as an influence technique to persuade the audience to take action. To achieve this will need to work on at least three dimensions so that you can realize your strategic communication objectives. This is because, as Daniel Kahneman notes in his book *Thinking Fast and Slow*, "associative memory" lies at the core of System 1. So the challenge you face here lies in making things believable for your audience, so that they think what you're saying is worth memorizing.

This book provides you with the framework to accomplish just that through STC. The difference between the STC framework from other methods is that it's holistic and has you work on memory in three dimensions. When you can influence what is retained and ensure that is believable, then what you are presenting becomes intuitive to audiences. Once this happens, you can influence the masses as humans constantly and instantly build a coherent interpretation of what's going on around us through our intuitive form of knowledge, which is stored in our memory and can be accessed without intention or effort.

So, what are the most effective techniques that you can adopt to create memorable content? To understand those techniques, we first need to understand how memory works.

According to one study, most people can remember an average of 3-4 things at once without turning to any memory aids in the process (Rouder et al., 2011). This is why things like social security numbers and phone numbers are broken into three or four chunks. With a bit of enhancement through memory aid techniques in presentation, you can make the mind recall an additional one to two things. That's why, as you'll discover later, we have our 5i Framework built around 5 ideas. What all this means is that unless your audience is made of memory champions, you need to design your story for the average person and assume that you need to focus on 5 things. As such, when writing decks or presentations, an extra effort should be given to a maximum of 5 ideas or takeaways from your story deck. The basic idea here is that ultimately, you would want to invest extra effort in key takeaways, such as the 5 messages and/or visuals that you would want your audience to remember. You should therefore make these 5 slides or messages memorable.

Keep the number of main ideas you present in a deck or story to five or less.

Memory Techniques

Rather than diving into neuroscience and the mysteries of how the brain makes and processes memory, I will keep the focus on some experiments and memory techniques that you can make use of. The techniques that I suggest here are based on extensive readings of books and papers on the subject of memory, and here I intend to give you what matters and the background to why I chose this approach.

What I am about to suggest is simply based on reverse engineering certain memory techniques for deployment into STC. To that end, I have chosen techniques that have been shown to work on the masses, and most importantly, on ones that worked best for me as I presented to audiences and yielded the best results as I experimented with different approaches throughout my career. In my experiments, I observed first-hand which techniques worked best in the context of STC and improved my audiences' ability to recall what I wanted them to memorize by the end of the deck. I then expanded these tools to make them actionable strategies for STC.

The first thing you need to be aware of when creating content is that your audience is not going to make an effort to memorize and retain it. Instead, it is your responsibility to make your content that's memorable for your audience, so that in the end, they will remember it as vividly as they can and for as long as possible. That's why you are deploying these memory techniques.

One of my favorite memory methods is the memory palace, which is based on an ancient memory technique, often referred to as the Method of Loci (Qureshi et al., 2014). It's my favorite because it combines several techniques into one.

The way the Memory of Loci works is by adopting a simple three-step process:
- Pick a space in an intimately familiar place.
- Develop a journey in your mind of the space you picked.
- In the back of your mind, place things you want to memorize throughout the journey into space in sequence.
- As you place these things into that space, associate each thing with a weird emotional, visual, and vivid context.

Memory champions who adopt the Method of Loci usually associate content with vivid elements in a familiar physical space such as a house, room, building, cities, etc. through the journey of the mind. The reason space and location are strong memorable dimensions in our brain is because as hunter-gatherers, human survival depended on the human ability to remember where in the vast land things like water, shelter, and food. Through evolution, that part of the brain developed so that humans have now become able to store the location information in physical space for easy retrieval on demand. Hence, if you have picked (1) your office as the space, (2) made the journey walking out of your office, (3) used the list of acronyms that I introduced earlier as per below, and (4) the vivid associative context, you will be using the Memory Palace effectively.

Here's an example of how you might remember various elements of STC using Memory Palace:

Acronym	Description of What to Remember	(3) Location	(4) Vivid Associative Context
3DF	The Three Dimensional Framework	Your Desk	The family picture on your desk contains your son wearing AR goggles and he's watching you run in circles across the 3 axes.
DSP	Descriptive Solution to a Problem	The Door	The chairman of the company climbing a ladder, wearing carpenter workwear trying to figure out a stuck automatic exit door.
ROT	Rule of Thumb	Reception	The receptionist is actually Mick Jagger giving you a "thumbs up" on your way out.
STC	Storytelling With Charts	Janitor	On your way out and as soon as the elevator arrives, the janitor decides to tell you the same story of his life when the door opens.
TA	Taking Action	Elevator Button	The elevator has only one button in English that says "Take Action" while all other buttons are in Japanese.
TUG	The Universal Goals	Destination Floor	The elevator door opens, you find yourself floating in space with 2 planets lit up and you need to figure out how to reach them.

Acronym	Description of What to Remember	(3) Location	(4) Vivid Associative Context
TBI	The Big Idea	Thinking Hat	You look around and don't know what to do, and suddenly a floating "Porte Chapeau" with a hat saying "The Big Idea" thinking hat approaches you in space.
5IS	The 5 Ideas	Choices	You put the thinking hat on and suddenly you get not one, but 5 ideas all at once, and don't know which one to choose.
DAN	Dopamine, Analytics, and Narrative	Three Things	It turns out you need 3 ingredients to reach your destination and get out of space. All 3 of them are in your possession: A book titled the "Narrative", a pill of "Dopamine" and an "analytics" app on your phone.
HL	Horizontal Logic	Journey	You find a sign that says train station that uses a "Horizontal" hyperloop to the 1st planet which defies "Logic".
VL	Vertical Logic	Journey	A rocket launcher that flies only "Vertically" and "Logically" takes you out of space and into planet earth and your final destination.
5SUF	The 5 Ideas	Stairs	You crash land on the rocket's released capsule on planet earth and survive by a hair. To get there, you find a "5-step" stairs (not a ladder) inside the capsule which has the slogan, "The Universe is a Framework".

Acronym	Description of What to Remember	(3) Location	(4) Vivid Associative Context
TVMA	Time, # of Variables and Message Attribute	Time and Intelligence	You look at the "Time", and you find that you arrived earlier than you departed. But you find yourself quite a bit smarter as your mind is capable of processing a large "# of Variables" and associating them with "Message Attributes" all at once.

Having considered this table, let's evaluate what, precisely, might be considered to be "memorable." Obviously, what I consider to be memorable is what happens during this journey, but the events that transpire while that journey is unfolding may not be as memorable for you. For example, you may consider commuting to and from work via train to be memorable. You may find other actions and visuals to be far more memorable, making the process that much more vivid for you. If this is your first time hearing about the Loci method, then all this information might be a bit overwhelming for you, rather than memorable. Of course, the main point of this example is neither to get you to memorize this whole list instantly (although it would be good for you to do so) nor to practice the Loci method. Rather, it's to illustrate how this method works, which I hope I've managed to achieve.

How to Make Memorable Content in STC

The first thing you need to remember when creating content is that your audience is not going to make an effort in remembering or memorizing your content. The good news is there are several ways to make content memorable for your audience, even if that's the case. The question here is what techniques work best and how could they be adopted in the context of STC?

Let me illustrate this with an example from business concepts. Business concepts are abstract, so as a general rule, what works for business is likely to work for anything. Let's consider a very popular visual example in the business world called the "2x2 BCG Growth Share Matrix." This visual is a simple two-dimensional 2x2 matrix that goes along two axes: Market Share and Growth. These lead to four buckets, each with its unique metaphor known as question marks, star, pet often represented by a dog (or underdog), and cash cow (Henderson, 2022):

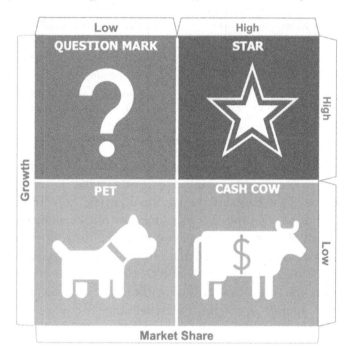

This framework was developed by Alan Zakon and Bruce Henderson in the 70s. It was so popular that it is still taught to this very day in portfolio management courses and as a management tool for executives who are looking to view their business units from a value perspective. For example, businesses with high growth and high share are considered "Stars" and could have the best future prospects, while low growth and low share businesses are the "underdogs" and should be considered for divestiture or liquidation.

The idea of the 2x2 matrix is similar to space visualization in the memory palace, and the growth-share name is mnemonic, which we'll get into next. The stars, cows, pets, and question marks are the odd and vivid associative objects related to action or outcome within a framework. This combination of space and vivid objects is what makes this framework memorable. The idea of the framework is that, once understood, anyone can recreate it from scratch if needed. After you've seen this for the first time, it becomes hard for you not to find it interesting and recall it later.

Putting abstract concepts into frameworks works by "Dimensionalizing" your content in simple digestible visuals that are easy to retrieve from memory. This is one of the key features of STC. It's the art of turning boring text into memorable space/place visuals. This technique is primarily adopted in Qualitative Charts, where you would use a memorable visual to explain, simplify abstract concepts, and improve the audience's ability to memorize it, so that you can refer to it later in your presentation deck.

Another good technique, which has already been discussed, is visualizing content. In a professional presentation, you cannot lead the audience into the space journey that I showed you earlier in the example of an acronym table. However, there are techniques you can adopt in visualization to increase vividness and memorization.

For Horizontal logic, narrative and storytelling are, in and of themselves, memory techniques. Despite this, associating stories with something that the audience can relate to can be more powerful than telling stories the audience are unfamiliar with. For example, you can draw on nostalgia as a powerful emotional trigger technique and link the stories that you are telling to something that the audience can relate to.

For vertical logic, the most effective technique works by adding emotional triggers to images. This can be accomplished in one of two ways: creating tension, and relating to metaphors. Creating tension, which will later be discussed in more detail and also mentioned in sections of the book discussing emotions, is a scriptwriting technique adopted by experienced copywriters and designed to keep the reader hooked as they're taken on an emotional roller coaster through story arcs at the story level (horizontal logic) or at sentence or paragraph level (headlines and vertical logic).

A very powerful technique that requires more creativity than others is the use of memorable metaphors. Some people are better than others at relating to metaphors, when possible. Such a technique works wonders in making your audience retain your content in long-term memory. While some studies show that visuals are better than words for memorability purposes, other studies have found that in certain contexts, words are more memorable than pictures (Ally & Budson, 2007). This is particularly true when they're used in certain contexts such as relating to metaphors and familiarity (Curran & Doyle, 2011). It's not important to argue either way, since STC is based on the combination of text and visuals. The important, therefore, is to learn the best way to leverage this combination to improve the audience's long-term retention. To do that in the context of STC, we will need to apply a mix of universally proven techniques that relate to the story deck to enhance retention.

Chunking is another technique that relies on grouping things in a memorable way. The STC framework does that automatically if you follow the horizontal and vertical logic in the upcoming chapters.

The use of mnemonics and acronyms is another popular memory technique. There are several sub-techniques and they are commonly used in strategy consulting. Sometimes they are3 referred to as the model mnemonic techniques which involve converting complex and abstract things into a framework using a construct or a model such as the BCG growth-share one described earlier. This technique is also expands into phrases, acronyms, numbers, rhymes, music, and images that are used in advertising slogans such as using catchy phrases like "Just do it" "Melts in Your Mouth, Not in Your Hands" or word substitute for numbers such as making it easy to order flowers in 1-800-Flowers or contacting FedEx 1.800.GoFedEx.

Let's take the example of a visual framework that was introduced in the Logic and Reasoning shown above as a 2x2 matrix. While this is a good illustration of potential strategic options for sales growth, I wouldn't exactly call it memorable. So, how can we apply the Loci reverse-engineered method to it to make it more memorable?

If the 3D visual effect that I created does not make it too easy to digest, we can simply turn this into 2x2 like the BCG Growth-Share matrix. Thus, it will become the Products-Markets Scope & Scale Matrix for revenue growth.

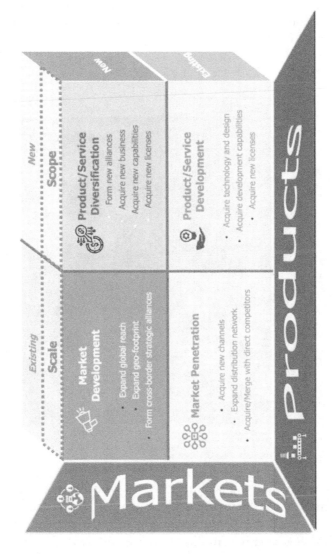

The basic idea of the techniques adopted in this example can be summarized as:

- Adopt a two-dimensional space that
- groups the possible options into "chunks" of four categories to choose from, based on 3 inputs (i.e., product vs. market, new vs. existing, and scope vs. scale).
- assign vivid, weird or memorable context to them using images and combine that with emotional triggers and tension (i.e., Russian Roulette and a smiley face).

- and gravitate towards a single option by inducing positive emotions and rewarding anticipation.

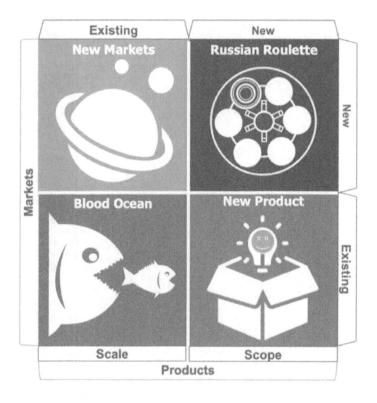

From the icons that you see in the visual, you'll notice that I chose a positive emoji in the "new product" category. I did this because if I were presenting to an audience and wanted to recommend such an option, I would choose a negative emotion icon for the remaining three options and leave my audience with a positive emotion to discourage them from the remaining three. For example, I could have also replaced the "blood ocean" with a "Swiss army knife" indicating the endless number of strategies that can be adopted in increasing sales.

On a final note, you should remember that repetition is an important part of making content memorable, which is why by the end of this book, you probably won't remember this visual as I won't be bringing it up again, since the context of this book is not about growing sales.

3DF Complete Picture

Now that we have introduced these techniques, we can complete the full picture of the 3DF by pairing two dimensions at a time which will lead to three strategies. The memorization of the key content can be achieved by combining engaging narrative with emotional content, as you know. Motivation can be achieved by combining emotional triggers with logic. Cognitive ease, meanwhile, is achieved by making analytical content easy to understand and interesting to absorb through narrative and engaging content, and as just discussed, memorization is achieved by developing content that is both emotional and engaging.

Then again, the idea of the 3DF visual provides you with a comprehensive, but also memorable visual that combines the rules and techniques that should be followed in STC. While I am not asking you to memorize the whole thing in one go, I do recommend, you save it as a visual on your phone so that you have a quick reference on hand, until such time that these techniques become second nature to you during content development.

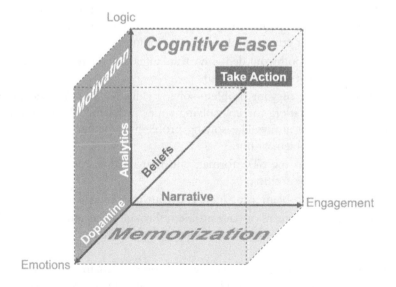

For those of you who are more 3D space challenged, we can draw this in one-dimensional format by expanding the content of the earlier introduced Venn diagram as follows:

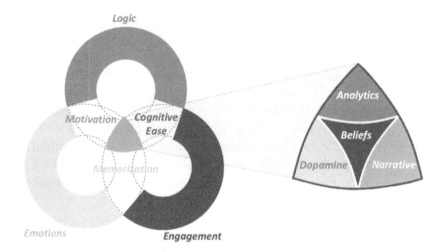

Recap

- You shouldn't spend too much time trying to understand your audience but you should spend time trying to understand all the different objections that can be raised to your claims. This way you can prepare to counter them effectively.
- If you can convince the most skeptical person in the room of what you're saying, you can convince your entire audience. To do this you'll need to make use of your critical thinking and reasoning skills.
- You should use both your deductive thinking and inductive reasoning skills to test your claims and your proofs.
- Follow the logic of your problem-solving skills to structure and draft an effective presentation, thereby solving your "problem." Presentations and decks are almost always like solving problems, whether your audience is aware of the problem or not.
- To tell a story in the STC format, you first need to establish what your context and goals are first.
- Structure your problem using logic and your reasoning skills.
- Identify the root causes of your problem through logic and reasoning skills and come up with possible recommendations that address these root causes.
- If you want your audience to take action, you need them to remember your content. To that end, you need to create memorable content. Most people can remember only three to four things at a time. You can increase this number by one or two more things by using certain memory techniques.
- The memory techniques you can use to increase audience recall are memory palace, the x2 BCG Growth Share Matrix, content visualization, adding

emotional triggers to images, using memorable metaphors, grouping things in memorable ways and repetition.

- Analytic encompasses the analysis work that needs to be done to complete a story deck. It serves two different purposes. The first is to guide your analysis. The second is to tackle beliefs. This latter requires engaging System 2 consistently throughout your story to reassure the logical brain that the story is not all fluff.

- The narrative is what brings your analytical story to life. You can have the best story in the world but without a good narrative, it can very easily become a flop.

- The right and left sides of the brain need to be tackled with 3DF.

- Statements not backed by proof cannot be presented as absolutes, that is if you want to hold onto your credibility.

- Disproving a claim is typically easier to do than proving it.

- The proofing mechanisms you can make use of are social proof and benchmarking, analogy proof, mathematical and analytical proof, demonstrable and visual proof, and undeniable facts that need no proof.

- A good story creates a sense of trust between you and the audience and makes suspension of disbelief possible.

- To evoke the feelings you need to evoke in your audience, you need to play on heuristic and system 2 to steer your listeners' brain chemicals in the direction that will get them to take action.

- You have to help your audience anticipate a pleasant reward at the end of your presentation.

- Cognitive biases can actually cause two people looking at the exact same data or charts to arrive at completely different conclusions.

Chapter 3: Vertical Logic and the Vocabulary of STC—A Formula for Life

Logic is the anatomy of thought. —John Locke

Warning! The following is a spoiler for the movie Benjamin Button:

The year is 1918 when Thomas Button abandons his infant son on the porch of a nursing home. This baby has been abandoned because he was born looking exactly like an elderly man. Luckily, one caretaker at the facility takes pity on him and takes him in. She raises him as her own, and duly names him Benjamin. As Benjamin grows in size, he continues to look like the patients populating the nursing home, despite being only a child. Despite this, his physical condition seems to reverse as he grows up. In other words, he ages backwards, getting younger and younger with each passing year. The older Benjamin gets, the younger he looks.

Around the time that Benjamin starts looking at a suitably young age, he meets the granddaughter of one of the nursing home residents and falls in love. Luckily Daisy, the woman in question, returns his feelings and the two get married. After Daisy gives birth to their daughter, however, Benjamin leaves them, thinking that he cannot be a suitable parent, given the fact that he's still aging backward. Ten years later, Benjamin goes back to his wife looking like a much younger man and he and Daisy get back together. At the end of the movie, Benjamin reverts back to a toddler, showing early signs of dementia, before he vanishes from existence completely (Fincher, 2008).

This story, as odd as it sounds, actually is quite similar to the Lindy effect, which is another kind of reverse aging phenomenon, though there are some key differences.

Lindy vs. Benjamin Button

Lindy's Law, otherwise known as the Lindy Effect, was first explored in an article published in the June 13th issue of the New Republic. The article, written by Albert Goldman, explained that "the life expectancy of a TV comedian is proportional to that total amount of his exposure on the medium" (Goldman, 1964). The article had gotten its title from a deli in New York City called Lindy's Eatery, where comedians would "foregather every night to conduct post-mortems on recent show biz action."

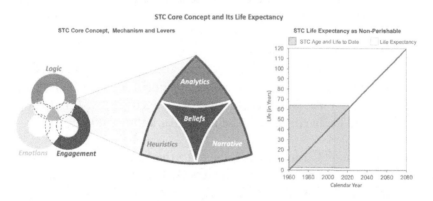

The Lindy Principle, which Goldman laid out in his article, later inspired numerous papers and textbook references and turned into a powerful ROT. In his 1982 book *The Fractal Geometry of Nature*, Benoit Mandelbrot dubbed the phenomenon the Lindy Effect. Mandelbrot claimed that according to the Lindy Effect, the more appearances a comedian made the more appearances they expected to create (Benoît Mandelbrot, 2006). This idea continued spreading, until it was infecting popularized bestselling books like *The Black Swan* and *Antifragile* by Nassim Nicolas Taleb, who in fact dedicates an entire chapter to it in the latter of the two works.

So, what precisely is the Lindy Effect? Taleb explains the concept as follows (Nassim Nicholas Taleb, 2012):

"The first thing to note about the Lindy Effect is to separate between the perishable and nonperishable. The perishable elements have unavoidable organic expiration dates, such as humans, light bulbs, canned food, etc. Nonperishable would be those with no organic, inevitable expiration date."

To clarify that explanation, basically, the Lindy Effect dictates that certain things really do age in reverse. There are two different kinds of things that do this: perishable and nonperishable things. You can think of these perishable and nonperishable things as objects and content. For example, vinyl records, CDs, or DVDs are objects or technologies that are perishable. Content like music and video, on the other hand, are not. Neither are books nor the bible. A printed copy of the bible might be perishable, subject to the wounds of time as it is. Its content, however, is not and can be expressed in tutorial format or printed in even more copies.

The Lindy Effect is relevant to STC because the framework used in STC is nonperishable and in fact, shows signs of aging in reverse. This is due to the fact that it has survived, grown, and been in use for decades already and will likely continue to be in use for another 60 years.

What makes the STC framework subject to the Lindy Effect like this is that it is grounded on influencing beliefs. It leverages logic, emotions, and engagement to build stories using analytics, heuristics, and a compelling narrative.

How Did It Go in 40 BLC?

Before exploring the STC framework in greater detail, let's first recap how building STC–based decks used to work in the year 40 BLC, meaning before laptops and computers. Back then, STC followed both horizontal logic, seeing as it was made up of individual slides, and vertical logic, seeing as presenters had to create a deck of slides.

These slides would be designed in this painstaking way: First, a consultant would sketch a chart and the visual would go on a sheet of paper. A slide rule was used to perform the necessary calculations to execute this move correctly. The slide rule was perishable, of course, and therefore later came to be replaced by a calculator. Once the sketch was ready, it was handed off to the visual aids department. Here drafters would sit down at the draft table and transform the material in their hands into a paper-based slide. Using pencils, they would create visuals that didn't contain any written text. These slides would only contain lines, shapes, graphs, and charts at this juncture. The drafters would use compasses, scales, triangles, and protractors to draw all of these things.

Next, the prepared chart would be sent up to a typist who could type really quickly. This typist would fill the slide with words, whose font was 10 pt. Once finished, they would proofread the slide one final time. If they found any errors, they would cut out portions and fix them, before the decks were shared with clients. If the slides were going to be used during a presentation, then they would be produced in overhead transparencies.

Slide Deck Development in the Year 40 BLC

Fast forward to today and this process has changed greatly. Transparencies vanished from the scene more than three decades ago, as they were entirely perishable. Over time, they came to be replaced by computers and laptops. The process of preparing a deck, then, went from being wholly manual, with hand-drawn charts and all, to wholly computerized. Designs from scratch thus became a thing of the past. Most of the tools we use today to design presentations have design template features or use plugin apps to make chart creation an easy and simple process.

How about the content that went into the slides then? While its true presentations have received a bit of a facelift, with various colors and icons, the core concept of STC has essentially stayed the same these past 60 years. The process of creating slides got more efficient, which contributed to the growth of the trillion-dollar global management consulting industry. It was able to do so by making the process far more scalable and increasingly possible.

What this means is simple: the STC concept has been around for a while and isn't going anywhere, anytime soon. Again, I am obviously not referring to the software or format used in STC when I say this. Who knows, maybe we'll be presenting charts in Meta or AR in just a few years. I am referring to the concept of telling a story in vertical and horizontal logic, which will remain unchanged for years to come.

The main takeaway to make from this is that the methods outlined in this chapter worked back then, still work now, and are likely to work in the future. These are lasting skills, and this book is the only book on the market today that condenses these methods into a single, easy read.

Top-Down and Bottom–Up

The problem I have with the majority of my trainees is that they insist on beginning the process with the data, then move on to figuring out what the best way to visualize and insert it into the story is. It's true that doing this might feel like it's more intuitive. It's also true that most books, training, and methodologies focus primarily on the VL and brush over the HL and the overall story. But in doing so, they forget that HL is a prerequisite of VL. They also forget that identifying the data needs to be the second to last step in the STC process.

If that's the case, how come this book started with a chapter on VL before moving on to HL? The answer is simple. It's because VL is a prerequisite skill to HL. Hence, when applying the STC methodology, you start with HL first. Afterward, VL determines your chart's blueprint before you go on to mine for data.

As you'll discover later in horizontal logic, this process is what brings us down to vertical logic while horizontal logic defines the kind of analysis and data you need to make to back a claim or a message. In keeping with that, the last step in horizontal logic is defining the graphs and charts that are required for the story. This, right here, is the main focus of this chapter. Tackling this last step first, before covering the previous steps might seem nonsensical at first. But it needs to be done so that you learn how to construct the vertical before moving on to structuring the horizontal.

Going back to our earlier language analogy, you need to start any language learning process by learning the words moving on to constructing sentences. The fact is, a sentence cannot exist without words, just as words cannot be made sense of if they're not put into a sentence. Considered within those definitions the HL of your presentation can be thought of as "the sentence." The VL, on the other hand, can be thought of as the words. You don't need to start with the data, that is to say the letters, when you're learning the words nor do you need to let the letters guide you to what you want to say.

What all this means is that you need to move on to working on your charts only after you've identified everything you need. Developing a slide is a process that unfolds on two levels. Level 1 is what's derived from horizontal logic. Level 2 is the blueprint. Both these levels are conducted from the top-down, not the bottom-up. That means that you need to approach these levels by figuring out your plot first and collecting your data after. That way you will be able to hone in on what's relevant to you without having to go on a data mining sprint.

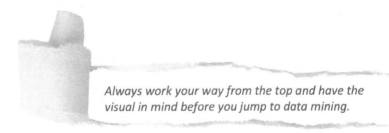

Always work your way from the top and have the visual in mind before you jump to data mining.

The Anatomy of STC

How exactly should you go about building your story with charts?

Rule number one is that you should always avoid working backward in STC.

The STC Framework Method

Horizontal Logic | Vertical Logic

The One Big Idea
- Goal
- Strategic Objectives
- Main Issue and Sub-Issues
- Hypotheses

Data — Chart
Identify and gather relevant **Data** to fill the **Chart** and answer **Key Question**

Blueprint
Select the most suitable chart **Blueprint** that answers the **Key Question** that proves your **Hypothesis**

Key Question
Ask the **Key Question** that leads to answers that can prove and validate the **Hypothesis**

Hypothesis — Headline
For each articulated best-guessed **Hypothesis**, proceed with vertical logic: headline message and chart design

The right strategy to adopt when building a story with charts is to begin by figuring out what your goal, strategic objectives, and big idea are. These will help you to identify the issues that set the framework of your storyline. They will make it possible for you to establish which claims and headline messages should be stated to articulate best-guess hypotheses.

This is why horizontal logic is considered a prerequisite of VL and needs to come before it. Horizontal logic is what defines your analysis and the data required to back the claims and messages of your story.

Always work your way from the hypothesis and claim and have the visuals in mind before you jump on data mining

The 99/1 Rule and the Double-Edged Sword

Does the name Altavista ring a bell? It should be, if you are of a certain age. In my day, when I was first starting out in my professional career, finding something even remotely useful when data mining or searching the web was an immense challenge. Enter AltaVista.

In 1998, the AltaVista search engine was used to operate on one of the most powerful computers in existence. This computer used 20 multiprocessor machines that utilized DEC's 64-bit Alpha processor. Together these back-ended machines had 130 GB RAM and 500 GB hard disk drive. They received about 13 million queries every day.

Though those figures sound like they're quite a lot, the truth is today we have more data on hand than the entire pool of content that the internet had to offer back then. All that to say, the internet wasn't anywhere near as big as it is in our current day and age. As such, when surfing the web we kept getting bombarded with pop-ups of pornographic websites, and finding the information that we needed was exceedingly hard. Finding useful and relevant data without coughing up thousands of dollars for industry and research reports was even harder.

In those initial years of my career, almost all the available data we had access to was either on the net or could be found in client databases. I rarely had to look beyond what was readily available. At most, I had to look at the occasional niche benchmark report or quantitative customer survey or focus group study.

In short, data has always been a bit of a problem in STC. In the past, the problem was that we had a scarcity of data. Today, the problem is we're absolutely submerged in it. This is doubly true for those of us who work for large companies and therefore get bombarded with data every day, most of which is either dark or pretty useless.

So, how are you supposed to deal with the paradox of differentiating between the data you need and the data you don't?

An ROT that will help you with this is that the most important skill you'll ever need for this is the ability to ask the right questions. By asking the right questions, you'll be able to sight through any size of data quickly and identify the 1% portion of it that really matters to you, rather than get distracted or become overwhelmed by it.

The most important skill you'll ever need is to develop the ability to ask the right questions

The Anatomy of a Chart and the Importance of Consistency

Two years into my consulting career, I found out that I was being put up for a promotion to engagement manager. The promotion had come into my sights much earlier than I had expected. Before the appraisal that needed to be done for the promotion, though, I was given a final assignment. For this assignment, I was reporting directly to Joe, a senior partner at the firm. The assignment was only supposed to last four weeks, even though the engagement in question would normally have taken eight to twelve weeks to complete with a team of two consultants, known as 2+1 in the consulting industry, working on it. To meet our deadline we had to work through the weekends and pull all-nighters. Proud of my output, printed the final version of my deck two days before my report was due and handed it to Joe to review. The following day Joe called me into his office and handed the report back to me with handwritten notes on it. His phone rang just then, so he asked me to check back in with him after reviewing his notes. I opened up the printed review and my heart nearly stopped when I saw that almost all the pages were marked in red, from top to bottom. I understandably freaked out, worrying how this would affect my promotion.

I had been in my position for two years and had mistakenly adopted the view that I had learned everything I needed to learn. I had convinced myself that I had mastered the art of STC. That, however, was not the case.

As I read through the review, I was relieved to see that most comments that Joe had given me had to do with the format I'd used. There were still some structural issues that had to do with the storyline (HL) which I needed to address though.

In working on the formatting issues, I learned a very important lesson: In the age of computer software and templates, there are no excuses for not having a consistent format on every chart. Inconsistencies were simply unacceptable in this regard.

What you should conclude from this is that every chart you work on has to have a consistent format across the entire deck. Luckily, you can ensure that this is the case by setting up and working with templates. While this book is not a software toolkit, you can still use the below guide to understand how you should set up your template. You can alternatively use the one that is provided and then customize it for your brand. If you want something other than that, you'll probably want to invest in a professional designer who will be able to prepare templates unique to you, based on the specs you provide them with.

Personally, I prefer designing my own templates for every engagement, seeing as this takes less than a couple of hours to accomplish. But my preferences aside, the simple truth is that a well-designed and simple template can save you a lot of time in the long run.

The core element in each and every chart you work on should be consistency. You should be consistent in everything from where various elements are positioned (how far they are from the left and the top, for instance) to the font size you use, the font color, and how elements like titles, headlines, labels, sources, notes, and page numbers look.

Consistency means, for example, that you can't denote the dollar by using the "$" symbol on one page and writing "USD" on the other. It means that you need to pick one and stick with it throughout the entirety of your presentation. Similarly, if a chart's numbering scheme is a single decimal point, then the numbering schemes of all the other charts in that same presentation should have a single decimal point as well.

Elements in a Slide and a Chart

A chart is made up of several elements. These elements can be referred to in a variety of different ways. As such, different firms may give them different names during on-the-job training. Regardless of how these elements are named though, the number of elements making up charts will always be uniform.

STC Framework Chart and Slide Elements

R#	Element	Visible	Must	Definition and Purpose	Design Rule
1	Headline	✓	✓	The main message on a slide extracted from the story	No more than 2 lines
2	Title	✓	✓	The description of a graphic or a chart within a slide	Consistent location across all slides
3	Chart Area		✓	The area in which the chart should fit and not exceed the margins allocated to it - as set by the guides set by this template	The area isn't marked but should be consistent throughout. Its borders should have the same distance from the top and the left
4	Ghost	✓		A text or graphic illustrating position in a story within the story	Can be a text, image or both and goes between the header and chart area
5	Label	✓		Description of highlights and visual cues	Location should be consistent across the entire deck
6	Ribbon	✓		Ribbons can be used to highlight an attribute or something on the entire slide. Can also be used for disclaimer (see below)	It needs to go above the header
7	Disclaimer	✓		Used to clarify and delimit the scope of proof in the chart that is used to support the headline claim or message	Disclaimers can refer to a specific chart or the entire chart area. Multiple disclaimers can be added
8	Callout	✓		A callout is a text or a visual cue designed to stress or highlight a particular message in the chart	Avoid overcrowding the slide

R#	Element	Visible	Must	Definition and Purpose	Design Rule
9	Page #	✓	✓	Is a must on every page except the first page	Format and location should be consistent throughout
10	Source	✓	✓	The source of the chart or the data in the chart should go on every slide. Every chart should have a source, i.e., if you have 2 charts from different sources, include the 2 sources	Consistent location, font, size, format at the bottom of the page but above the footer if there is one. Separate different sources with semicolons
11	Footnote	✓		This is a useful field to explain or justify specific elements, figures, analysis, etc. in the chart area	Use only when clarification or qualification is needed. Usually comes before the source field listed in numerical order and use 10pt font or less
12	Note	✓		Unlike the footnote, the note typically refers to the entire chart and not specific elements within the chart.	Comes after the numbered footnote if there are any
14	Footer	✓		A footer is only needed for branding, or adding disclaimers, copyright and confidentiality marks	It's recommended but may crowd out the slide
15	Margins		✓	The position and the space and margins between the elements in the chart including the headline, the title, and the source/note field	Positions of titles, internal charts (i.e., for a single chart or multiple charts), margins, spacing between elements and the spacing from the top and the left should be consistent throughout

The charts above provide you with the names and definitions of the most common chart elements. Where you place these elements in a chart isn't exactly set in stone because the only thing that matters when it comes to these elements is consistency. If you have remained consistent across the board, then the template you're using should be uniform in placement, color, fonts, and image sizes throughout your entire presentation.

The reference numbers (R#s) in the tables are visualized and illustrated on individual slides in the examples that follow.

The "Visible" column in this visual indicates whether a specific element or rule is about a visible element or not. The "Must" column, on the other hand, denotes whether it should apply to every single content slide in a deck.

The Relationship Between the Elements on an Individual Slide

One of the ROTs of STC is that you should only have one message per slide in VL, if you recall.

Contrary to what most people think, presenting two ideas on a single slide takes the exact same amount of time that presenting them on multiple slides takes. If you are not constrained by the number of slides you can use—which you should not be—you can certainly split your messages into different slides. In doing so, you can keep from cramming multiple messages and charts into a single slide. Doing this will generate fewer questions and make your overall message easier to digest for your audience.

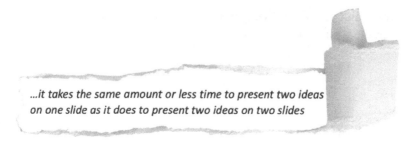

...it takes the same amount or less time to present two ideas on one slide as it does to present two ideas on two slides

Whatever claim you're making or insight you're sharing should be explained in a one, at the most two-line, single sentence in your headline. That claim or insight should be fully supported by your data and the analysis that can be found in the chart that is located in the body of the slide.

There's a symbiotic and almost recursive relationship between the headline message and the body of the slide. This is because the body of a slide supports the message and the message dictates what the body should contain. Something mentioned in the headline shouldn't be missing from the body. Likewise, something mentioned in the body shouldn't be absent from the headline.

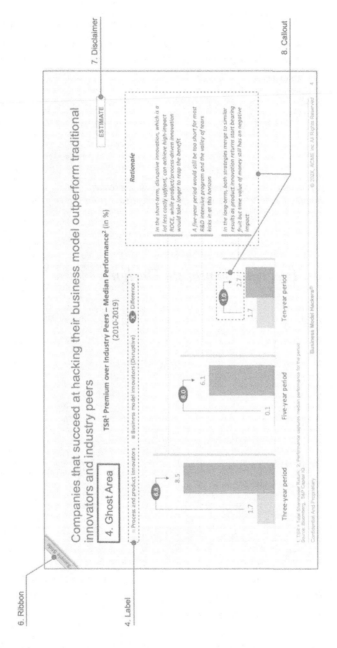

That being said, slides aren't exactly chicken and egg situations. Your message always comes before your chart is selected, as mentioned previously, and determines the chart or visual that will be required to support it.

One ROT you should keep in mind is that you should be able to accurately guess what your headline has to say if you were to hide the headline and view the chart by itself. For the record, the reverse of this statement is also true.

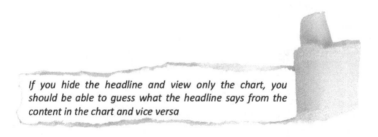

If you hide the headline and view only the chart, you should be able to guess what the headline says from the content in the chart and vice versa

The Look, Feel and Template Design

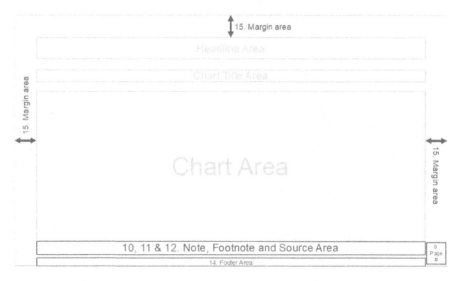

Whether you outsource your slides to a designer or not, having a template to work from is something that can ensure that all the chart rules remain uniform across your deck.

For reference, a template is a predesigned blueprint for your slides that contains your branding, fonts, layout, colors, and the like. In PowerPoint, templates can be viewed under Slidemaster.

R#	Element	Visible	Must	Definition and Purpose	Best Practice Design Rule
1	Date (for Data)	✓		If you have data on the slide, the date of the data is essential to indicate on the slide	If the data is not actual, or consists of a mix of actual and estimate, the date should include a letter to designate whether it's an estimate or a forecast
2	Units	✓		The units of the number is essential to include and	Consistency in how to use the unit across the deck. In addition, e.g., if metric is used, the entire deck should be in metric
3	# of Digits	✓		Numbers displayed should be consistent and have no more than 3 digits, preferably 1 decimal point	This should be consistent across all numbers in the deck
4	Font Type		✓	The best practice is to have one type of font across the entire deck	Font type should be chosen in the template
5	Font size		✓	Is the size that is set across all text elements in slide. Including, the header, titles, chart content, text boxes, etc.	Size should be chosen in the template and should be consistent across the entire deck
6	Colors	✓	✓	Set a color palette and stick to it. Avoid the use of excessive colors	Set the color scheme to be the same across the entire deck
7	Template		✓	The template sets the position of the lead in, the margins, the color palette, the fonts, etc.	It's a essential to work off a template, no matter what software is being used
8	So What?		✓	A question to be asked at the end of every slide to ensure it addresses the story's objective	Ask before and after the slide is completed: What is the purpose of the slide? Is the takeaway clear from the headline? Does the slide address the story's objective?

Templates are pre-saved for frequent use and quick access. You can create custom templates, store them, reuse them, and easily share them with others.

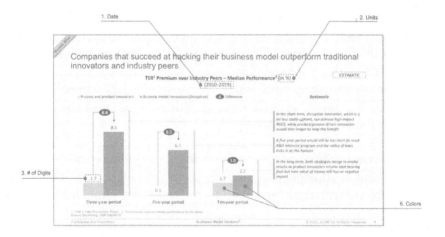

You can get fancy with templates too and add different layouts and additional elements to them. If you want to gain access to the most commonly adopted templates available on the market and the ones that are used by MBBs, you can take a look at them in our toolkit.

An ROT to keep in mind is that the fewer pages in your templates, the better and the more consistent your deck's "look and feel" will be.

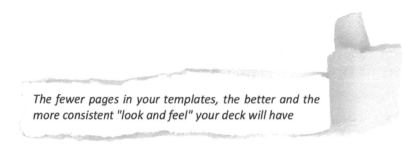

The fewer pages in your templates, the better and the more consistent "look and feel" your deck will have

One rule you can never go wrong with is less is more. As such, the focus of STC should be put on something other than fancy layouts and colorful slides. Instead, itt should be on insights, story, and on backing your claim with absolute credibility. Focusing on these things first and foremost always works like a charm.

At least it has for me. Granted, some situations may call for more colorful decks and images, such as inDesign, storyboards, concepts, and illustrations. But the possibility of the very occasional exception doesn't negate the fact that your story always needs to be backed up by analytics and logic. Given that, your slides always need to be simple and get straight to the point, even if your analytical model and data analysis require more complex modeling.

The core concept here relies on simplifying your findings into something that any kind of audience can instantly absorb through vertical logic and that can be presented to them with just a handful of templates.

The must-have templates in any presentation are the title slide, the table of contents, the blank page, and the single-page chart. You can maybe include the double or triple chart page templates in this list as well.

Over time your library of reusable charts will grow as you keep building more presentations. What that growth will look like will depend on what your business and profession are. Soon you'll start pulling charts from other presentations and customizing their headlines. You'll also start customizing those charts, so that they fit in well with their new homes, instead of starting charts from scratch with every presentation.

Whether you are presenting virtually, onscreen, in a hall, or in a conference room, you can use the following chart table to guide your font size, assuming you're employing the standard Arial font.

Best Viewing Distance by Screen Size			
Font Size (in pt.)		Screen Width	
		3 meters	4 meters
Can you read this?	9	3	3
Can you read this?	10	3	4
Can you read this?	12	4	5
Can you read this?	14	5	6
Can you read this?	16	6	7
Can you read this?	18	7	9
Can you read this?	20	10	15
Can you read this?	22	12	17
Can you read this?	24	15	20
Can you read this?	28	17	24
Can you read this?	32	20	26

Considering how much the work environment relies on technology these days, the fact that computer screens have become the standard presentation format shouldn't be a surprise. That being the case, that smaller fonts are seldom legible during presentations shouldn't be a surprise either.

Despite this, I would recommend that you use 10 pt. fonts in all your slides, except for their Footer, Source, and Note sections. As for colors... You might think that is of secondary importance but you would be wrong. The color you use in your presentation will be linked to your brand, after all. If you find that you struggle with colors, you can send your template to a professional designer. They can then develop your sample slides based on a chosen color palette. Alternatively, you can build your own color palette using the colors of the main logo you've been provided with and by applying different shades to them throughout the presentation.

If you have a single-color logo or brand to work with and insist on using more colors, a good strategy would be to find matching color combinations through a simple online search. If, on the other hand, you're working for a client who prefers adopting internal branding to the presentation, you should combine black and gray shades with your slides' main brand colors.

The Four Types of Charts

There are two kinds of slides that are usually included in every deck. These are "fillers and bloaters" and "appendices and backup slides."

Fillers are the types of slides that include the Table Of Contents (ToC), agendas (see example below), separators, or chapter slides. I refer to separators as using their secondary name, bloaters, because I'm usually not a big fan of them. Bloaters, however, are a necessary evil, especially if you're dealing with a big report made up of several phases of work streams, really long presentations, or workshop presentations.

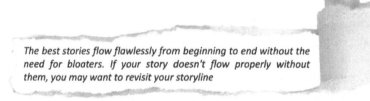

The best stories flow flawlessly from beginning to end without the need for bloaters. If your story doesn't flow properly without them, you may want to revisit your storyline

Despite this, though, you should remember the ROT that the best stories flow flawlessly from beginning to end without the need for bloaters. If your story doesn't flow properly without separators, you may want to revisit your storyline.

Meanwhile, appendices are those slides that aren't necessarily a part of the story but could be referred to as backup materials or analyses supporting the specific messages that the main story gives. They're the executive summary presentations and backup charts you have on hand, just in case you're asked for them or in case you need to demonstrate how you arrived at a specific claim you're making.

In addition to all these, there are also your approaches and your framework charts. These are your structural, skeleton charts. Structural charts form your foundation. They're the spine that holds most and sometimes all of the storylines together. In my estimation, though, these can be considered bloaters as well. This is because they can be counted as smart replacements for ToCs and agendas, which brings me to qualitative and quantitative charts.

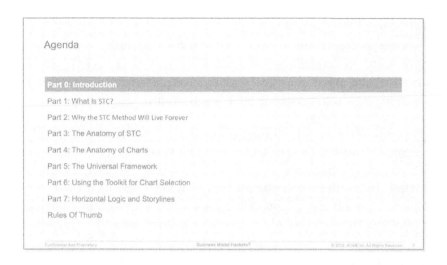

Qualitative and quantitative charts are the last category of charts that can be included in slides. These charts are what make up a story when they're used in a specific sequence.

The Distinction Between Stories and Storytelling

Before we can venture into the world of VL design and development approach, we have to establish what the distinction between stories and storytelling is. Your deck and its HL are what you use to tell your story, as we have established. When you run through your deck, your story should flow in the way you want it to. At the same time, every chart contained in your deck should be a story contained within itself. The well-known metaphor, "a picture is worth a thousand words" therefore feels oddly fitting for STC. If you're making a short presentation of 10–25 slides, for instance, every chart in that slide should be a self–contained story.

If your horizontal logic is your main plot, then your vertical logic can be considered your sub-narratives. They make up short stories, scenes, and moments that add details and value to your overall plot. It's hard to express a full and complete story on a single slide in visual format if you are not doing a voice-over narration over it. This is why we have to distinguish between in-person presentations vs. executive summary decks accompanied by an in-person presentation.

Understandably storytelling is much easier to do in the in-person or voiceover presentation format. This format literally gives you the opportunity to explain what each slide and your overall story is indicating and what message they're given. It reduces the risk that something will become lost in translation or difficult to grasp.

Compared to the in-person format, the deck–based storytelling without voiceover is much more difficult to do. This is because you have to make sure you communicate every message you mean to give clearly, and concisely but without missing anything when using this format. If you prepare a poorer deck, you risk things becoming lost in translation, without you there to provide voiceover explanations and clarifications.

The Universal Framework for Vertical Logic

Most STC methods are taught to trainees to focus on vertical logic. This is because VL is the most straightforward concept you can learn in STC. You neither need any kind of special training nor need to read really long, thick books to master VL. All you really need to do is master some basic rules that you can quickly memorize or sum up on a handy cheat sheet, which you can use until this information becomes intuitive or second nature to you.

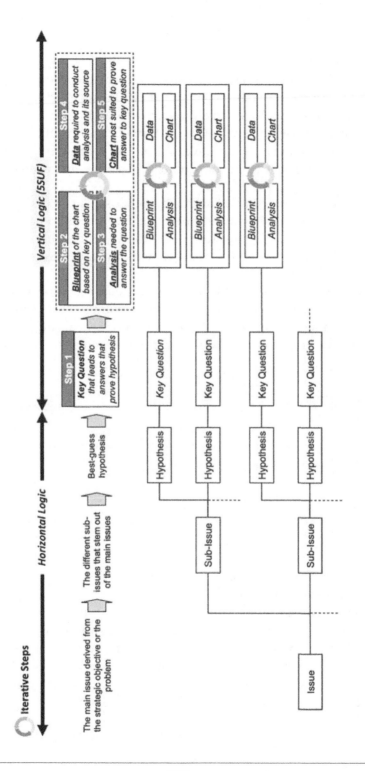

A core STC skill for you to make note of is how HL design is used in structured thinking. You can make use of several mental techniques and methods to structure your thinking abilities. One such technique is called the issue diagram. Alternatively referred to as the hypothesis-driven approach, the issue diagram has you formulate a hypothesis based on what issues or sub-issues you have on hand. You, of course, derive these issues and sub-issues from your strategic objectives and main goal.

Assuming you have come up with a hypothesis, your next step is to ask the right questions so you can prove that hypothesis to be correct. In the issue diagram, you can break down the VL into a simple Five-Step Universal Framework (5SUF) that can work for any chart.

As you'll recall, the horizontal leads to individual claims or messages. In the case of the issue diagram, your starting point is a series hypothesis. Why hypothesis? Because you have yet to prove them, and you need to build the verticals you need so that you can demonstrate each of them.

Hypothesis – Question Example

Issue: Sales and profits are declining	
Sub-Issue 1: The company is losing market share to new entrants and competitors	
Hypothesis	**Question**
The technology adopted in the company's product is old dated and undesired by customers	Is a new or emerging technology replacing the old one?
Growing attrition of users who are switching to substitute products	How many customers switched over the past three years? Where did customers purchase or switch to?
Product prices of like-for-like features are too high	How do the product prices compare to competitors' products for the same features?
Users are increasingly dissatisfied with the product	Are users unhappy with our product?
A new product launch is required to retain customers	What happens to our sales or financials if we don't launch a new product and the current sales trend continues?
A new state-of-the-art technology will be required to remain competitive	If the company copies a competitor, wouldn't it be just playing catch up?
Acquiring a new company or startup in a new emerging technology space is one of the best and quickest ways out of the vicious circle	What are the options to get out of this vicious cycle and how do these options compare to each other?

Now that we have established all this, let's take a closer look at how this universal framework works. As you can see in the given issue diagram, the vertical design is actually an iterative step. The first step in the framework is the key question. The key question is a fixed point. The second and fifth steps of the framework, on the other hand, are not fixed. They're iterative as well. Before delving deeper into each and every one of these steps, let's clarify how 5SUF works and to differentiate between what quantitative and qualitative charts are:

5SUF starts with the hypothesis. From there you develop your key question. This is step 1. Next, you answer that question in your headline, which helps you to develop your blueprint. This is step 2. You can now use your blueprint as a guide for your analysis, which will in turn narrow down your data requirements for you. That is step 4. Finally, the narrowed down and chosen data will be displayed in a compelling visual in the form of a chart, which is step 5.

Moving on, quantitative charts—the primary focus of this chapter—are data and number-driven charts. Qualitative charts, on other hand, are visuals that are primarily text-driven.

Quantitative or Data-Driven Charts

One thing I always tell my trainees and apprentices is that you should only go for qualitative charts if you cannot find the numbers and quantitative data to back claims or messages. You should always aim to drive your story forward using quants and have as many quantitative charts on hand as possible to back your full story. This is because arguing with numbers is harder to do than arguing with more abstract data. The numbers that drive a given chart and thus drive a specific story often says it all, so long as you pull the right numbers to support your claims and headers.

Claims that are supported by factual data and solid reasoning are more compelling than claims supported by subject matter experts, focus groups, or other qualitative evidence. Therefore, an ROT you need to bear in mind is to let the quants drive your story and prioritize quantitative slides over qualitative slides.

Let the quants drive your story, and always prioritize quantitative slides over qualitative slides. Remember that numbers speak louder than words.

That being said, some people take this advice a little too far and go overboard with data visualization. Doing so can be tempting, as it will give you an opportunity to show off your technical skills by choosing the most complex visuals available. This, however, will be counterproductive to what you want to do. What you should be doing instead is prioritizing simple charts as discussed earlier, since they will always be accepted as proof.

Step 1: The Key Question

There is a quote that's often attributed to Albert Einstein: "If I have an hour to solve a problem, and my life depended on it, I will spend the first 55 minutes determining the proper questions to ask, for once I know the questions, I could solve the problem in less than 5 minutes"

Whether this quote was really said by Einstein is unimportant. What is important is that it demonstrates how solving problems is all about asking the right questions. In our case, where vertical logic is concerned, the problem we're trying to solve is how to support the claims we're making and the messages we're giving in our slide's headline.

Accomplishing this requires proving our hypothesis. We don't need to worry about how our hypothesis came into being at this stage. Instead, we need to focus on the questions we need to ask so that we can either prove or disprove our hypothesis.

When recruiting new people to our industry, we try to find those candidates who are able to ask necessary questions like this. When we recruit or interview strategy consultants from top MBA schools, we screen for candidates who demonstrate an ability to think strategically. We do so by checking if they can come up with the right questions when solving problems in case interviews.

The importance of structured thinking may not be blatantly obvious at first. This doesn't change the fact, however, that every aspect of work and life revolves around our ability to effectively structure our thoughts, plans, and data. This kind of thinking requires quite a bit of discipline because, as humans, we intuitively think about many different things simultaneously.

The final step in the process is data analysis and selection, which can be guided by the answers you give to the questions you ask, designed as they are to prove the hypotheses you've made. Asking the right questions, then, is a core skill you need to learn across all levels, starting with HL, meaning the entire story, down to all the individual messages that make up the story, meaning VL.

To show what this process might look like, let's take a hypothetical example:

Suppose that your issue is that your company is losing market share to new entrants and competitors. You can come up with any number of hypotheses explaining this situation and even more questions that could be asked about them, as exemplified in the chart below.

Quantitative Chart Selection Universal Equation

Chart Type = F(T, V, MA)

T = Multiperiod = From the Past Until Now

•We are Gaining Market Share•

V = 2 or More = Us + Competitors

MA = Comparison of Us vs. Them

Symbol	Variable	Explanation
T	Time Variant	Is there a time factor, meaning is it static in time or trending over time? The answer is yes or no
V	Number of Variables	Is it a single or multiple variables? The answer is the number of variable, i.e., 1, 2 3 or more
MA	Message Attribute	What is the insight that needs to be shown? i.e., is it a comparison, breakdown, relationship, distribution or frequency?

Step 2: Blueprint

Once you have asked your questions, you can move on to step 2, which is the blueprint phase. The blueprint is the methodology you use to select the type of chart you'll need in the early stages of your work. This is the most important step of 5SUF as it sets its scope and the focus of both the analysis and data mining processes.

You might be tempted to use qualitative charts at this stage, as always. But you should remember that numbers always tell a better story than verbiage does. So, unless you work in the legal field, you should always be able to rely on quantitative charts and numbers to back most of your claims.

As an ROT, let the quants drive your story, and always prioritize quantitative slides over qualitative slides. Remember that numbers speak louder than words.

When selecting which chart or data to use to illustrate or back the claim you're making, start with the claim or the eventual headline that you derived from the hypothesis, as well as the question you asked in Step 1 of this process.

Use the following formula when selecting your chart:

Chart Type = F (T, V, MA) where

T= Time, V = Variables, and MA = Message Attribute

You determine T (time) by establishing whether the issue at hand has a time factor. It either does or it doesn't. You determine the number of variables by establishing whether you're looking at a single variable or multiple variables. You'll be able to find the answer to that question in the form of the number of variables. Finally, you determine the message attribute by asking yourself what the insight that needs to be shown is.

Fundamentally speaking, there are five attributes you need to consider when working to identify which type of quantitative chart you are to use. These are hierarchy, breakdown, frequency, relationship, and comparison.

This formula is referred to in STC as TVMA. The secret to identifying which chart to use lies in deciphering the message and determining what the value of the three variables in the equation are.

As an example, let's say that your message or claim is "We are gaining market share."

This message implies that we are comparing yourselves to our competitors over a specific period of time, stretching from the past till today. This means that:

T = There is a time component to this equation.

Variables = "Us" + competitors, which means that we have two variables.

Message attribute = Comparison, seeing as our market share is being compared to that of our competitors.

There are a total of 16 families of charts that you can use to visualize almost every quantitative scenario you can imagine:

The 16 Families of Charts

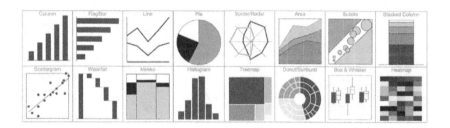

Using both "icons" and texts, his visual clearly shows how the answers you uncover using your equation can be plotted into your chart blueprint. So, if you were to use the flowchart for our market share example, you would begin your work by identifying your message attributes first. In this case, this is "comparison." Then you'd move on to time, which is changing as opposed to static. Finally, you'd identify your variables, which you have two of. You can then use this information to determine which of the chart options is the best fit for you. In this case, the flag chart, bar chart, or the line chart would be viable options for you.

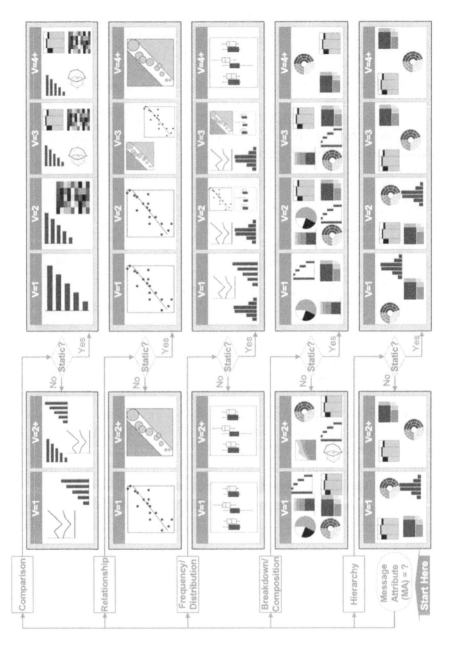

Additionally, you can use the table format below to determine which type of chart is best suited for which type of equation component. As you gain experience though, you will find that you've started committing this information to memory, until it becomes intuitive at last.

TV► / MA▼	Static: Single Point in Time				Trending: Changing over Time	
	1 Variable	2 Variable	3 Variable	4+ Variable	1 Variable	2+ Variables
Comparison	Flag	Multi flags Heatmap	Mekko Multi flags Spider/Radar Heatmap	Mekko Multi flags Spider/Radar Heatmap	Line Column	Line Column Flag
Relationship	Scattergram	Scattergram	Bubble Surface/3D Scattergram	3D Bubble	Scattergram	Bubble
Frequency/ Distribution	Histogram Single line Column	Multi histograms Multi line Scattergram Box and Whisker	Multi histograms Multi line Bubble Box and Whisker	Box and Whisker	Box and Whisker	Box and Whisker
Breakdown/ Composition	Pie Waterfall Stacked Column Treemap	Multi-stacked column Multi pie Mekko Donut/Sunburst Waterfall Treemap	Multi-stacked column Mekko Donut/Sunburst Waterfall Treemap	Donut/Sunburst Treemap Mekko	Multi pie Stacked Column Waterfall Donut/Sunburst Treemap Mekko	Area Donut/Sunburst Multi Radar Waterfall Mekko
Hierarchy	Donut/Sunburst Treemap Histogram	Donut/Sunburst Treemap Mekko Multi histogram	Donut/Sunburst Treemap Mekko	Donut/Sunburst Treemap Mekko	Donut/Sunburst Treemap Mekko Multi histogram	Donut/Sunburst Treemap Mekko

Step 3: Analysis

Analysis is the step you use to ascertain a hypothesis' validity by doing data mining and finalizing your chart. The analysis is a kind of computation that you may need to do on your data set. Doing analysis can require something as simple as creating an excel sheet where datasets are reorganized so that they can fit into a chart. It may also be as complex as working with dynamic or optimized models.

Complex modeling is something you typically only have to do if you actually want to do it. For instance, it can measure the impact of a particular initiative or recommendation. It can also test out different assumptions and possible scenarios and can be used when you want to optimize a goal like increasing company valuation or profitability based on varying multiple assumptions or input.

On the whole, measuring the impact your recommendations have is usually a good idea. However, seeing as most analysis is usually made in the form of an assessment, going over the four common sense methods often employed in analysis is a good idea. If you want to learn even more about these methods, then all you need to do is a simple web search. It's important, however, that you remember how most of the analytical work in the STC framework relies on common sense, rather than your ability to use some complex, magic formula.

The First Method: Fermi Thinking

Fermi thinking is an estimation technique that gets its name from the physicist Enrico Fermi. It has been adopted to solve extreme problems that cannot be easily resolved through mathematical or scientific means.

Fermi thinking allows you to arrive at a solution by adopting answers and using them as orders of magnitude estimates. Put in layman's terms, Fermi thinking has you break down problems into smaller chunks and then divide those chunks into two piles you'll label as "known" and "unknown". This allows you to become aware of what you know and what you need to learn. You can then use what you know to figure out what you need to learn (Chakraborty, 2020).

Fermi thinking, then, is a quick and simple way of developing a frame of reference for what you might expect your answer to be. As an ROT, and in the context of data validation, you should apply Fermi thinking where applicable, to check if the data at hand is within a reasonable range.

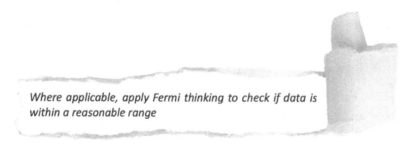

Where applicable, apply Fermi thinking to check if data is within a reasonable range

The Second Method: Data Triangulation

Triangulation is a term that has been derived from the Latin word "Triangulum". Within the context of data mining, it's the metaphorical reference you use to validate how accurate data points are. You do this by examining the data from different points and then cross–checking them with various data sources.

The Third Method: The 80/20 Rule or the Pareto Principle

You might already be family with the 80/20 rule. If you're not, then I would suggest doing a quick search online as this is an important tool to have in your arsenal. So much so, that it's also an ROT for when you're analyzing independent data sets like assessing how product defects are caused by 20% of the issues in the production line. The 80/20 rule basically says that 80% of the problems in any given scenario are derived from 20% of the causes (Tardi, 2022). By virtue of its logic, this rule can be used to figure out and focus on what matters most in a given situation. That might be fixing 20% of the problems at hand, since by fixing them, you'd be eliminating 80% of the issues you're having anyway.

The Fourth Method: Sensitivities and Scenarios Analysis

Sensitivity analysis is an analysis that's made by analyzing the movement of a specific metric under different values. By contrast, scenario analysis is an analysis that's made by analyzing the movement of a specific metric in different scenarios (CFI Team, 2022).

The key difference between the two is that scenario analysis tries to predict the future value of something, like say an investment. Sensitivity analysis, on the other hand, looks at how the outcome of decisions changes when the ongoing variables change. One of the most important things you can do when you're evaluating several data sources is to stress test your analysis. In other words, it's to consider how sensitivities and variance impact your hypothesis and see if they cause it to change in any way.

An ROT to remember is that you should run both types of analysis if you have a variance at hand, so that you can see whether your claims hold up or not.

Technique Name	Fermi Thinking	Data Triangulation	The 80/20 Rule and the Pareto Principle	Sensitivities and Scenarios
Origin	Named after physicist Enrico Fermi	Derived from Latin, "Triangulum"	Named after the civil engineer Wilfredo Pareto	Often used in financial modeling and simulations
Description	• An estimation techniques adopted for problems are extreme and cannot be solved mathematically or scientifically • The solutions involve adopting the answers as an estimate that is an order of magnitude. The Fermi estimation gives a quick, simple way to obtain this frame of reference for what might reasonably be expected to be the answer	• When sourcing data, it's often the case that different data sources have conflicted data sets • Triangulation is a metaphorical reference to validating the accuracy of data points by examining the data from different angles and by cross-checking the sanity of each data source and how it was obtained	• Pareto distribution is easily modeled in a spreadsheet and graphed on a powerful but simple two-dimension graph visual. It reveals major insights in large datasets and complex problems, systems and programs. It's also a simplified visual of power law distribution • It's a good rule of thumb to assess and determine the 20% area of focus or quick wins	• One of the areas to test when validating hypotheses with data are the assumptions made to lead to the conclusion that the hypothesis is valid • Sensitivities and scenarios allow the stress testing of how variances in assumptions can affect your conclusion and thus the confidence in the proof of your hypothesis
Use Case Examples	Used to check if data is within a reasonable range	Use to validate and more accurately select data sets from multiple sources	Used to understand structure of dependent datasets or for prioritization and focus	Used to stress test the robustness of forecasts, conclusions, claims, etc.

Step 4: Data

The truth is, you might not always have to use data for every single presentation. But since quantitative charts are more powerful and effective in proving claims than verbiage is, using data won't ever hurt.

Unless you're working on a legal-based deck, numbers always speak louder than words. That said, having legal proofs and claims sprinkled throughout your slides can actually benefit your STC. This is because they increase engagement and structuring, as you'll see later in the qualitative charts chapter.

For now, the key question to consider about quants is whether you have the numbers you need to back your claims and when you should put them together. Your numbers should ultimately hold and validate your claim and hypothesis. If they don't, then you may need to re-evaluate them. If they do, then you need to assess your data using the following criteria:

- source credibility/authority
- relevancy
- accuracy
- completeness
- recency

Having several ways to back up a claim is always a good idea. Given that, repeating steps 2 and 3 of the Universal Framework once you've finished collecting your data can only reinforce your choice of a blueprint. It can also boost the confidence you have in your proof and evidence before you move on to the last step, which is to finalize your chart. Having several data sources will also enable you to gather the evidence you need to prove your claim.

As you go about this process, though, you should always remember that acquiring data can sometimes be tricky. You should also remember that it's not about how much data you've been able to gather. It's all about the process of identification you've used and the quality of the data you've obtained.

Step 5: Chart

Step five is when the old saying "a picture is worth a thousand words" finally becomes realized. This saying couldn't be truer for vertical logic. Hence, the chart you pick should reflect your message without saying it in words.

An ROT to remember here is that the fewer words you use to make your claim or message come to light, the better your chart will be.

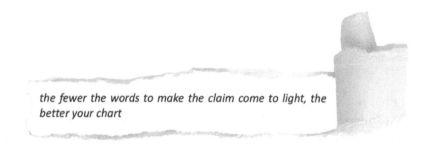

the fewer the words to make the claim come to light, the better your chart

Once you're done mining and analyzing data, you'll have to finalize the visualization of the chart you've selected. This is the easiest part of the entire process because it's the part where everything falls into place.

It's worth mentioning, though, that the TVMA blueprint may lead you to multiple chart blueprint options. Sometimes, it may lead you to as many as six different possibilities. That is perfectly alright. If and when you end up with multiple chart options, you'll be able to choose the most suitable one based on which data and data sets are available to you.

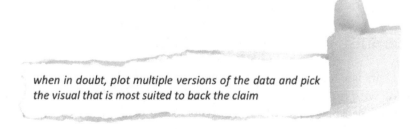

when in doubt, plot multiple versions of the data and pick the visual that is most suited to back the claim

Another ROT to remember then is that you should plot multiple versions of the data and pick the visual that is most suited to backing your claim.

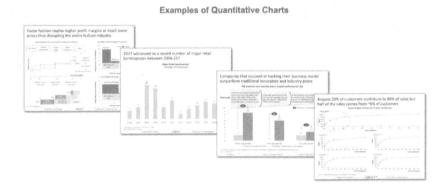

Examples of Quantitative Charts

As a final note, oftentimes you might have to combine several charts under a single headline or claim. Once you've mastered how the family of 16 charts are used, you'll be able to mix and match different ones without issue and use chart combinations easily.

Visual Cues

What would happen if you were to turn a flashlight on while outside, on a sunny day? The flashlight would have little to no effect and would basically be useless. Using chars that don't have any visual cues to focus the reader on the message it's trying to give would be the same as turning on a flashlight, outside in broad daylight.

Visual cues offer several advantages when used in vertical logic and charts. Of these, three are particularly important within the context of STC. The first of these advantages is that visual cues, particularly ones that aren't easy to interpret, help guide the reader's focus to the part of a chart that reinforces the message its headline is trying to give.

How can you use visual cues to accomplish this? You can do so by playing with font sizes, colors, and shades, as seen in the example below. You can also make use of icons, which have become quite popular in recent years. You shouldn't use icons excessively, though, seeing as this would reduce how effective they are as cues.

You would be able to induce visual cues far more effectively if you were to use a laser pointer or pen to point things out to your audience during a presentation, if you're

The second most important advantage that visual cues have to offer is the fact that they can serve as memory cues. Memorability is a very important STC as you want your audience to remember the important points you make. In other words, you want high audience retention. Visual cues can be very memorable in and of themselves and thus increase retention. At the same time, they can get your audience to act by having them recall the things you presented later on.

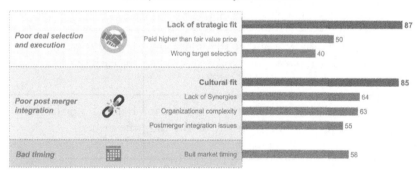

The Top Three Reasons Why M&A Deals Fail

The third most important advantage is chart interpretation. To see this advantage at work, consider the phrase "I didn't say he stole the cash." If you read this phrase without emphasizing any of the words, nothing about it will grab your listener's attention. It'll simply mean that you didn't steal anything. But if you were to stress the words "say" or "nothing" in the sentence, then you would be giving a whole other meaning, complete with the "wink, wink, nudge, nudge" kind of indication. Stressing different words in a sentence, by making them ***bold, underlined, or italicized,*** for instance, can achieve this same result in presentations and open up your charts to greater interpretation as can be seen in the example below.

The key takeaway here is that the meaning of your chart can change based on what you choose to emphasize. The same goes for visual cues, in that how and where you use them can help you to emphasize different parts of a chart. Using certain kinds of colors or shades in a chart can add some life to your vision and enhance the meaning you're giving to it. Color should not, however, be used as a part of your core messaging. If a chart shows that one variable occurs more often than another, for instance, it can make the bars showing this for these variables different colors. This would emphasize the difference between the bars but the key message the bars give would be conveyed through the fact that they are of different heights.

Stress Word	Meaning	Read
I	She is trying to say that she is not the person who said the man stole the money. Somebody else said it.	*I* didn't say he stole the cash.
didn't	She is trying to say that she is not the person who said the man stole the money. Somebody else said it.	I *didn't* say he stole the cash.
say	It sounds like she wanted to suggest that the man stole the money. But she did not want to say it directly.	I didn't *say* he stole the cash.
he	It's suggesting that someone else stole the money, not the man identified in the sentence.	I didn't say *he* stole the cash.
stole	It might mean that the man just borrowed the money. Maybe he didn't steal it.	I didn't say he *stole* the cash.
the	The speaker is suggesting that she is talking about some other money, not the specific money that is being discussed.	I didn't say he stole *the* cash.
cash	The indication is that the man stole something else. For example, maybe he stole jewelry or some other valuables.	I didn't say he stole the *cash*.

When you're working on charts, keep in mind that some executives still prefer working on and with printed paper and don't always print out the presentations given to them in color. This means that you might work on a chart and emphasize certain parts with colors but those emphases would be lost if the person you give your presentation to prints it out in black and white. Add to that the fact that there are 300 million people across the world who are colorblind and that 4% of the US population is colorblind and relying on colors in charts becomes a decidedly poor idea (Clinton Eye Associates, n.d.).

Qualitative or Conceptual Charts

Qualitative charts, sometimes referred to as conceptual charts, are used to visualize the dense text in a structured format. As mentioned previously, you can build a good storyline using a combination of mainly quantitative charts and a few supportive qualitative charts. The obvious exception to this rule, of course, is fields that rarely have to rely on numbers like legal advisory.

A legal advisor would have to prepare a deck or presentation that may be entirely made of text content. If they're working on something like case studies, they'll have to rely less on numbers as such studies don't have a lot of quantitative charts but have plenty of qualitative ones.

So, how can you convert verbiage into slides without risking audience engagement?

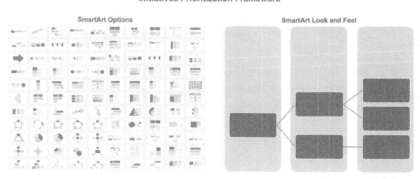
Initiatives Prioritization Framework

The most recent version of Microsoft PowerPoint has attempted to build such visuals under the "SmartArt" option. However, the options provided here, unfortunately, lack the flexibility you need to have in freeform art like this. Of course, there are software tools and add-ons you can turn to add automated freeform versions of this art onto your deck. Personally, though, I have yet to find a tool that is flexible enough to amend the shapes I'm provided with into freeform ones.

If you have purchased the toolkit on the Story Telling with Charts website, then that means you now have access to 2,000 freeform qualitative charts. You can quickly select these charts using a simple cheat sheet and add your chosen visual to your slide in minutes.

Qualitative Chart Categories

In the meantime, you should know that there are several categories of qualitative charts. The visual below has grouped these together by name and provides you with the most common ones. The categories that qualitative charts fall into are:

- **The Text to Visual Metaphors:** These are the most common charts. They are simply variations of the same concept. You convert text into a concise and nice visual to keep the user engaged. These also include table charts.
- **The Conceptual Frameworks:** These are explanatory charts that illustrate intellectual concepts visually.
- **The Story Flow Framework:** These are simple, flowing charts used to guide the reader through a complex deck or a storyline within a storyline.

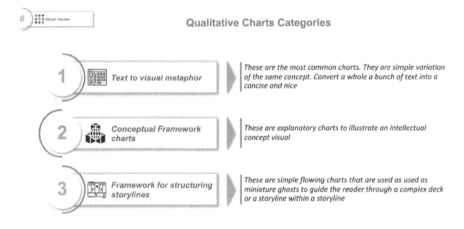

The Text-to-Visual Metaphor Qualitative Chart

The purpose of a qualitative chart is to convert text and paragraphs into mentally engaging visuals. Of course, there is some science, that is to say, a method to the madness of accomplishing this.

Text-to-Visual Metaphor Examples

Visual Illustration of Corporate Business Unit Portfolio Distribution

Cash Flow

Mature Businesses / Annuities

Growth Stocks

Experiments / Options

Age

	Entry	Development	End State
Goal:	Market entry, learning	Strategic differentiation	Market leadership; market driving positions
Issues:	Options renewal, innovation pipeline	Resource constraints; Growth expectation	Annuity rate drop; Tradeables vs. strategic core

Business Unit Portfolio Management Strategies in the Form of a Lookup Table or Cheat Sheet

Yield Create Level / Portfolio Basket	Options	Growth Stocks	Annuities
Margin Plays (Market Discontinuities)	Can we supercharge the upside by buying assets with significant optionality? Which businesses may grow faster than market?	In which sector and geographies can we accumulate assets at the bottom of the cycle?	Which markets will experience precipitous margin decline positions are tradeable?
Strategy Plays (Competitive Discontinuities)	Where are we experimenting to define the next strategic leadership play and which innovations will define future market leaders?	Which markets offer big bang opportunities from leveraging our strategies and where can we redefine the rules of the game in large markets?	Where are we the undisputed market leaders, able to set the terms of trade?
Turnaround Plays (Operational Discontinuities)	Can we enter somewhere advantageously by buying or turning a wedding around?	Where can we roll-up or fix weak competitors?	Which under-performing mature businesses offer the potential for market leadership and are there any mature business units worth fixing?

Unlike other qualitative charts, the number of metaphors that can be adopted in this type when visualizing a text are endless. The sky's the limit in terms of which visual you can adopt as a metaphor.

The most experienced presenters usually use the same kind of bullet point or picture slides when running through text presentations or slides. However, you should avoid bullet points at all costs in STC. Otherwise, you'll end up boring your audience to death and preventing engagement.

Instead of using bullet points, you can make use of different types of art and thus add a bit of liveliness to your deck. In doing so, you can increase engagement and content retention.

To simplify this process, I have summarized the most common and popular metaphors you can use. While the list is not exhaustive, it should be enough to inspire any kind of messaging. Thanks to this inspirational cheat sheet, you should never run out of ideas for visuals to keep your audience engaged.

It's important to emphasize, however, that the visual itself is less important than the structure your qualitative argument follows in a qualitative chart. The process of structuring and organizing your main messages is the key to solidifying your VL.

So, with that in mind, how do you go about crafting your visuals? The first thing you need to do is to structure or organize your content before putting it into slides. To that end, ask yourself:

- What are my main themes and ideas? How many main themes or topics are there? What's the best way to group the content?
  - o Grouping the content into themes enables you to determine the number of elements you will need in the visual.
- Do all the themes link to the main message or claim?
  - o o If a theme or message does not support your headline or claim, then it should be removed.

Conceptual Framework Charts

Conceptual framework charts are explanatory charts designed to simplify how an intellectual or complex concept is illustrated in an easy-to-grasp visual. This is often referred to as a framework.

The best way to explain conceptual charts is by example:

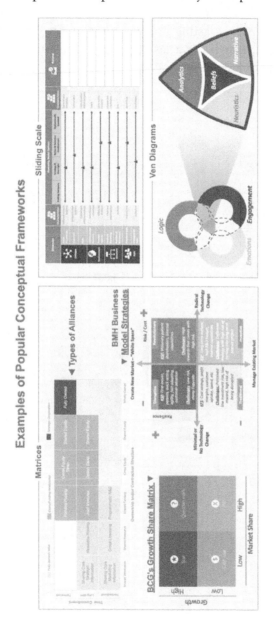

Matrices and Categorization

If you've already come across the famous 2x2 Growth Share Matrix developed by Boston Consulting Group (BCG) in the 70s BCG, you know that the concept is simple. It's so popular that it is still in use and is frequently referred to in business to this very day. This shows how simplicity can leave a lasting impact and why this category of charts, if well developed, can leave a lasting impression on your audience and become a memorable experience for them.

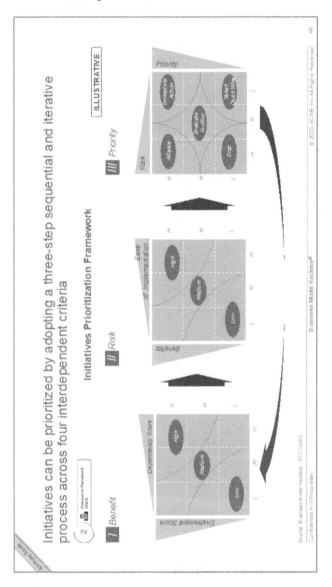

The BCG matrix has four quadrants (Hayes, 2022b):
- low growth, high share

- high growth, high share
- high growth, low share
- low growth, low share

This simple categorization system can help you to categorize a variety of data and values. You can then determine which to drop or which to take immediate action on, for instance, based on which quadrant they fall into. In keeping with that, the above example shows a 3x3 matrix that can be used in a sequence.

Ranges, Comparisons, and Evaluation

The conceptual framework can be used in many areas, as it operates on a sliding scale.

We define we kinds of operating models for corporate structures, each suited for a different level of control

Level of Control

Lowest ——————————————————————————————→ Highest

Type	Holding Company "We just want to know your results"	Strategic Oversight "We want to know what you do"	Active Involvement "We want to know how you do it"	Operationally Involved "We will work with you to do it"
	Lowest	Medium-Low	Medium-High	Highest
Mission	Meet corporate governance, fiduciary and legal responsibilities	Add value where the business cannot and leverage synergies between the Business Units	Provide direction/guidance and expert support to businesses	Run the enterprise essentially as one business
Leadership Activities	• Mandatory activities (e.g. governance, fiduciary responsibility, legal compliance and manage liability) • Provide strategic oversight • Acquire/divest businesses with a portfolio approach (risk, return, diversification) • Allocate funding to businesses	• Corporate wide activities which the businesses cannot provide for themselves • Give strategic, financial and value creation guidance • Oversee activities that span across businesses	• Proactive strategic guidance to businesses via expertise sharing • Proactive risk management and expertise services to businesses (e.g. capital, people, strategic planning, financial analysis) • Manage activities that span across businesses	• Active ownership of key strategic and operational decisions – limited business unit authority • All staff functions required to support decision making, e.g. Planning & financial analysis, business development, human resources, legal)
Rationale	• Value is created by individual companies close to customers • There are no potential synergies between individual companies	• Value is created by individual companies close to customers • Businesses present potential synergies at various levels (e.g. production, distribution)	• Value is created by individual business units using corporate expertise • Businesses exploit synergies at various levels • Co-ordination of business strategies is required	• Value is created by corporate expertise and control • Business lines are similar • The primary dimension of competition is cost / operational efficiency
Examples	Berkshire Hathaway, Carlyle	Alphabet, Procter & Gamble	Facebook, Coca-Cola	Walmart, Starbucks

Source: Business Model Hackers

For example, it can be used as a guide to select a model—in the above case an operating model. To do this the framework will have you define your scale, as shown above, and then use that scale to help you choose the adequate operating model for you, as shown below:

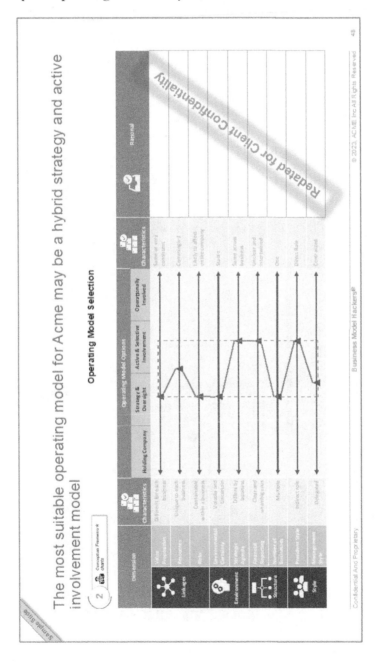

Alternatively, you can use the scale you have defined as a gap assessment tool, especially if you're evaluating how something is performing against the "best practice" in the industry or something of the like. The fact that these charts veer toward simplicity means that they can be designed as visuals able to make powerful analyses and deliver thorough insights.

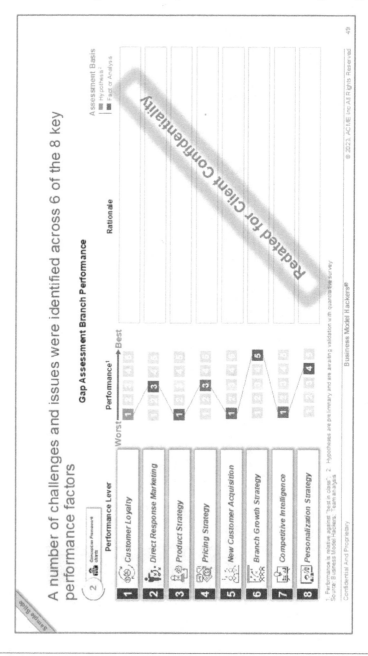

The Story Flow Framework

The structure visual is one of the most important visuals that can be used in any story. As per its name, it's used to structure the flow of either a whole story or of stories within the larger narrative. It's a better alternative to turn to than bloaters and separators, seeing as it helps maintain the horizontal flow without introducing any interruptions to it.

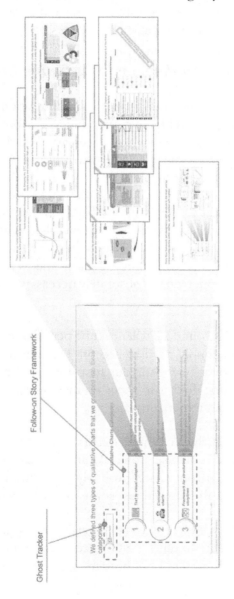

Qual Combo Charts

Qual Combo Charts include both qualitative and quantitative visualizations on a single slide. They are particularly useful in highlighting, expanding, and explaining the takeaway the audience is supposed to make when looking at a quantitative chart. They come in especially handy when the takeaway can't be intuitively interpreted by the audience. They also make sure that the audience is able to directly access the claim that is being made or the message that is being given.

Decluttering, De-Wording, and Finetuning Charts

If you want to improve your chart's communication skills and make them as engaging as possible, then one thing you absolutely have to do is declutter and de-word them where necessary. The risk with qualitative charts is that they can come to be overly wordy and therefore distracting or overwhelming if we let them.

Start the decluttering process with the headline message, then move on to your data and slides. Select the kind of visuals you want and fill in the text as needed. Then go over the written content once more and try to see if you can word anything more concisely and clearly, without losing your message. Consider what is absolutely necessary to convey and what can be let go of.

The first version of your deck will never be perfect nor should it be. This is something you simply need to accept. This means that you do not need to agonize over how bad your first draft is. What you should be doing with your first draft is to focus on making sure it contains all the information it needs to contain, after all.

If you use templates that you purchased as part of the toolkit companion to this book or if you use PowerPoint add-ons like Think-Cell or Empowersuite, then your charts probably won't need to be cleaned up too much. Instead, they'll need just some minor formatting.

If, on the other hand, you are using PowerPoint graphs without plugins, then you will have to do quite a bit of decluttering on your charts. This will include removing things like borders, gridlines, and data markers.

Recap

- The Lindy Effect dictates that certain things really do age in reverse. There are two different kinds of things that do this: perishable and nonperishable things.

- STC is nonperishable and in fact shows signs of aging in reverse.

- You start STC with your horizontal logic first and then move on to your vertical logic, which determines your chart's blueprint.

- Your horizontal logic defines the kind of analysis and data you need to make to back a claim or a message.

- Always work your way from your hypothesis or claim and have the visual in mind before you jump to data mining.

- Always avoid working backward in STC.

- The right strategy to adopt when building a story with charts is to begin by figuring out what your goal, strategic objectives, and big idea are.

- The most important skill you'll ever need in STC is the ability to ask the right questions.

- Always be consistent throughout your presentation. Having a template to work from is something that can ensure that all the chart rules remain uniform across your deck.

- If you hide the headline and only view the chart, you should be able to guess what the headline says from the content in the chart and vice versa.

- The fewer pages in your templates, the better and the more consistent your deck's "look and feel" will be.

- The best stories flow seamlessly from beginning to end without being interrupted by bloaters. If your story doesn't flow well, you need to revisit your storyline.

- 5SUF starts with the hypothesis. From there you develop your key question.

- Next, you answer that question in your headline, which helps you to develop your blueprint.

- You can now use your blueprint as a guide for your analysis, which will in turn narrow down your data requirements for you.

- Finally, the narrowed down and chosen data will be displayed in a compelling visual in the form of a chart.

- You can make use of both quantitative charts and qualitative charts. As a rule, unless you're working in the legal field, you should try to use quantitative charts as numbers speak louder than words.

- When applicable, use Fermi Thinking to check if your data is within a reasonable range.

- When you're analyzing independent data sets like assessing how product defects are caused by 20% of the issues in the production line.
- Sensitivity analysis is an analysis that's made by analyzing the movement of a specific metric under different values. By contrast, scenario analysis is an analysis that's made by analyzing the movement of a specific metric in different scenarios. You should run both types of analysis if you have a variance at hand, so that you can see whether your claims hold up or not.
- The fewer words that make up your claims, the better the charts.
- TVMA blueprint may lead you to multiple chart blueprint options. When in doubt, plot multiple versions of the data and pick the visual that's most suited to it.
- Visual cues help guide the reader's focus to the part of a chart that reinforces the message its headline is trying to give and can serve as memory cues.

Chapter 4: Horizontal Logic— Story Structure Through Structured Thinking and Hierarchy

A system of logic must be composed, like music, of distinct parts which combine in a harmonious whole. –Augustus de Morgan

When I first started my career in strategy consulting, I thought I would roll up my sleeves and dive into business the same that I used to when I was working in the corporate world. Boy, was I wrong. On my first day on the job, I learned that the main deliverable that strategy consultants worked on was something called a "deck." A deck is a horizontal document made of hundreds of pages, summarizing the strategic and gap assessment made of a business situation. It's something that does a deep dive into that analysis and is an approach that takes place during an engagement. It provides audiences with the strategic actions that a business, entity, or organization needs to take to achieve the objectives they want to achieve.

Considering all the purposes a simple deck serves, I was very overwhelmed when I saw an example of one. This particular example was the result of a three-month-long engagement and contained over 500 pages of PowerPoint slides. Faced with such a document, anyone would be overwhelmed.

When I asked my then-engagement manager how I should go about building such a deck, he answered me with, "It's simple. What's the story you want to tell? Start with the story."

Speaking of stories… The year was 1896 when an Italian economist and philosopher and engineer, busy harvesting peas in his garden noticed something rather odd. He noticed that some of the peapods he was looking at contained more peas than the others. Intrigued, he started investigating the peapods by counting and sampling them and the peas. He found that, oddly enough, a small number of the peapods actually accounted for the majority of the peas produced. He also noticed that, if there were 100 peapods and 500 peas in total, a single peapod held an average of five peas in it. So, he selected the peapods containing the largest number of peas and found that 20 out of the 100 peapods in the garden contained 400 peas. The man decided to continue with his sampling and increased his sample size. Yet no matter how large his sample size grew, the percentages always remained the same in that 20% of the peapods always accounted for 80% of the pea output. No more and no less.

As you might have guessed by now, the man who was conducting this bizarre experiment with peas and peapods was named Vilfredo Pareto (Talent Stream, 2018). Being an economist and all, Pareto decided to see if this condition applied to fields other than the cultivation of peas. To his surprise, he found that it did. In fact, the 80/20 principle applied to many areas ranging from health, wealth, and even relationships, though to varying degrees. For instance, Pareto observed that 80% of the wealth of a country was typically concentrated on 20% of its population. Given observations like this, Pareto was later credited for discovering the power law distribution. Power laws are relationships where a minor change in the quantity of something results in a major change of another quantity (Bar-Yam, 2011). Power laws can be observed in pretty much all fields and aspects of life. For instance, if a small group of people are consuming the majority of the resources that a country, school, or health system has to offer, then that is an example of a power law.

The 80/20 rule, which is a kind of power law, isn't always exact. Regardless it's still an effective metaphor for the principle that a small percentage of something can account for a larger percentage of something else. This is an important concept to remember in the context of STC, as are power laws in general.

Moving on, the most important thing you need to remember and start with where horizontal logic is concerned is structure. That being the case, you might be wondering why this book didn't start with structure, but began with vertical logic instead. The simple answer to this is that you need to learn the words of the language you are trying to gain proficiency in before you can move on to structuring them. That way you can gain the proficiency you want faster. Now that you know the vocabulary you'll be using in STC, how do you go about putting them in order and structuring them?

Structured Thinking

A lot of the principles and concepts that you encounter in STC as things others can teach you. Structured thinking, however, is not, which is somewhat problematic because every aspect of your work and your STC needs to be structured properly. A number of training consultants have tried teaching their trainees all about structuring, as you'll discover momentarily, through vehicles like the Pyramid Principle and the Issue Diagram. But the fact remains, that potential consultants are primarily screened for their ability to think in "structure" before they can actually become consultants, since structural thinking isn't a teachable skill. Or at least, that is the general assumption that's made in the industry. I personally disagree with it. I say that anyone can learn structuring, which is the foundation of STC. The problem isn't that this isn't a teachable skill, it's that structural methodologies and frameworks are neither intuitive nor comprehensive. It's also that most books, trainings, and strategies focusing on the subject only cover part of the entire set of skills someone trying to master STC would need to have in their arsenal.

So, what's ultimately important in STC is the core structure. The structure is the very foundation of a presentation and it's what you always start with, first and foremost. Think of it like this: if I had to chop down a tree and was given an hour to do so, I would spend my first 45 minutes sharpening my ax. Then I would get to chopping, because a sharper ax would make my task far easier. Of course, this doesn't mean you have to devote an entire 45 minutes to figuring out your structure when you have an hour to finish a deck. What you'll spend the majority of your time on is data analysis, after all, so that you can go about building your charts, i.e. your individual messages. Still, this general idea is one that you need to bear in mind, especially now that you are better acquainted with the 80/20 rule.

If you were to apply the 80/20 rule to scale, you could say that you would spend 20% of your time on structure and 80% of it on things like data analysis and working on individual charts. Of these two things, though, the structure would be responsible for 80% of the success of your deck, whereas the rest would account for 20% of it.

With that in mind, what are some of the methodologies you can adopt to make sure you have a solid structure?

The Three Universal Goals (TUG) That Lead to Action

Strategy and management consultants have a bad rep for two reasons. The first is that they're often accused of taking your knowledge and feeding it right back to you. As the famous joke goes, "they take your watch to tell you the time" That's true to some extent, seeing as most of the data a strategy consultant works with comes from the client company. But analyzing that data in a relevant way by asking the right question, solving existing problems, and presenting them in a structured manner that enables strategic options and decision-making is a process that organizations aren't able to conduct internally. How can they, when they haven't been trained to do so?

The second reason consultants get a bad rep is that they are said to present clients with strategies that are out of touch with reality. Again, this is true to some extent. Take the GameStop frenzy which was discussed earlier on. As mentioned, in March 2022, BCG sued GameStop for $30 million for refusing to pay their consultancy bill. The ongoing case is a good example of the reality disconnect that can happen between client companies and strategy consultants.

That said, client companies tend to buy into the strategic recommendations and solutions that strategy consultants make more often than not. This is because, in the STC models developed by consultants, very little effort is put into influencing or persuading the client to take given recommendations.

When a strategy consultant is making a presentation to a client, they are telling a story that the client can buy into or not. Two universal goals apply to every story, regardless of what that story's specific goal is. The first is to get the audience to take action once the story concludes. That action could be anything from changing one's attitude to agreeing with certain findings. This is referred to as TA, as you'll recall. The second universal goal is to showcase a solution to an existing problem.

The Four-Step Approach to Perfecting Your Horizontal Logic

There is both an art and a science to the horizontal approach. To develop the skills you need to develop, you first need to understand the science. For that, you need a toolkit, an approach, or a universal method that you can then adapt when designing your structure. However, there is also an art to horizontal logic. If you liken HL to language, once more, you can see that different words can be strung together in different orders and make different sentences. Though these sentences might convey the same meaning, some will be better and more effective than others. The structure of a sentence can be changed up so that the same words lead to different meanings, reactions, and interpretations too, and herein lies the crux of the art.

Consider your speaking voice for a moment. A change in the pitch of your voice can alter the way you sound out a sentence. This can, in turn, change how your sentence is interpreted by your listeners' brains.

Articulating Strategic Goals and Objectives

To build a good structure and convey the right messages in your story, you need to start the process by crystallizing your strategic objectives. This is something you have to do before you can even think about tackling design and structure. To do this, ask yourself what you're trying to accomplish with your story? What is your main aim and goal? Picture your audience and ask yourself what you want them to take away from your story. This probably sounds quite easy to do. Unfortunately, it isn't. This is because your ultimate goal isn't necessarily the same as your strategic goal and objective. Your strategic goals and objectives are what you need to have in place in order to achieve your ultimate goal, after all.

For simplicity's sake, let's take boxing as an example. If you were a boxer entering the ring, your ultimate goal would be to beat your opponent. Your strategic goal, which will help you to win your match, would be something different though. It might be, for instance, keeping the bout going multiple rounds so that you can tire out your opponent. It might also be knocking out your opponent early on. Your strategic goals and objectives define how you're going to go about accomplishing your overall goal, then.

Like universal goals, you'll need to articulate each and every one of your strategic objectives separately. Otherwise, you will not be able to distinguish between them. Let's say that if you are pitching a product or service to a group of decision-makers at a potential new client company. The purpose of your pitch, in this case, is to get these decision-makers to purchase the product or service you're offering once you're done with your presentation. In such a case, this ultimate goal shouldn't also be your strategic goal. Think about it: if every chart in your presentation simply gave the message "buy my product," would the potential client be convinced that they should, indeed, buy your product or would they conclude that the pitch didn't offer them anything of real value?

If this is the case, then how do you articulate your strategic goals? Well, when working to phrase your strategic goals, you shouldn't really worry about things like the semantics, title, and how to best phrase your goals. There is a specific framework for phrasing these goals, of course, but we'll go into that later. What you should focus on at this juncture is what strategy you're going to adopt in your story to achieve your ultimate goal. Later on, this decision will drive your analysis and data compilation, as well as how you build your charts.

So, you start designing your structure by determining what your goal, strategy, and strategic goals and objectives are. Clarifying your overall objective in this way is important for several reasons. For one, it helps you focus your research and analysis on things that will actually be relevant to achieving your objective. In other words, it will make zeroing in on the proof and evidence you need a much easier feat to accomplish. For another, it will give you the ability to quickly qualify your content by testing whether it can sufficiently achieve your objective or not. If you find that it cannot, you'll be able to expand on your content through more proofs, examples, and analysis or even by finding better ones. Finally, clarifying your objectives will inform the tone you will be adopting throughout your pitch—formal or informal, for instance—as well as how to position the messages you'll be given in your slides.

Building a Comprehensive List of Hypotheses

Let's assume that you're in the private wealth management business and just happened to meet John Doe at a party one of your wealthy friends is having at their Upper West Side apartment in Manhattan. Based on these facts, you concluded that John Doe must be wealthy like your friend. This conclusion is really your hypothesis. The thing is, you wouldn't want to waste your time talking to John Doe and eventually pitch your services to him, only to find out that he isn't, in fact, wealthy and is therefore unable to afford your services. Instead, you'd want to maximize the time you're spending at the party by focusing on individuals who are potential prospects only.

But, how can you go about proving your hypothesis in this scenario? It's not like you can just ask John Doe whether he's wealthy or not. No, instead you'll have to don your Sherlock Holmes hat and do a bit of investigating. This way you can quickly figure out the approximate financial condition of Mr. John Doe and decide whether he could afford your services or not.

So, you've come up with a hypothesis after having a quick chat with John Doe. You built that hypothesis on the fact that he's wearing an Audemars Piguet wristwatch, has Prada shoes on, and has been invited to this exclusive party by your wealthy friend. While those are good indicators that you might be right, they don't exactly prove your hypothesis. Who knows? Maybe the branded items he's wearing are just really good fakes.

However, you work in wealth management, remember. That means that over the years you've built in a series of ROTs and investigative questions that can help you gather the evidence you need to confirm your hypothesis quickly. Whether you're actually at a party like this or in the office, working on your deck, this is the exact mentality you need to develop and either prove or disprove a hypothesis. You bring this mentality to your hypothesis, the key questions you ask about it—which was discussed in the VL section earlier—and the 5UF method which you use to obtain your proof.

Whatever your strategic goals and objectives may be, the one undeniable fact on hand is that you have a problem you need to solve. You can solve any problem, so long as you ask the right questions about it—something we've touched briefly on during our discussions of vertical logic. But there is a difference between creating a single chart that proves the message you want to give and identifying what the message you want to give is. This is why vertical logic is the lowest level of proof cascading up to your top hypothesis.

The best way to illustrate this situation is, again, through an example. Let's assume that you've been tasked with identifying why a company is losing money. To that end, you need to first come up with a hypothesis. One way to improve your hypothesis-building skills is to train your brain to think through different viewpoints and lenses. In other words, it's learning to think in alternative ways to come up with various reasons as to why a single event might be taking place. In the consulting world, that concept boils down to asking the right questions.

Horizontal logic and your storyline organization are like constructing a building. You start construction by laying down the right foundation, which will hold up the structure of your building. In HL, your foundation is your story's main idea. Your structure, then, is the series of sub-ideas building on top of each other and thus leading to, strengthening, and validating the main idea.

Developing a solid structure requires structured thinking abilities. One technique that can be considered to be part of these abilities is the issue diagram. The issue diagram, first referred to in the HL section of this book, is a powerful technique because of its simplicity. It is so powerful, in fact, that so long as you master this technique, you won't have to master any others.

The Issue Diagram

The issue diagram is both the simplest and the oldest method to be found in the strategy consulting world. It's great for helping you to structure your thoughts and for doing thought processing and analysis. This method doesn't help you develop your flow but it does help you identify the individual ideas and messages that will support it.

The nice thing about the issue diagram is that it is comprehensive and holistic. It also allows you to view the various connections that exist between seemingly separate issues and sub-issues. This is something that other methods simply don't do.

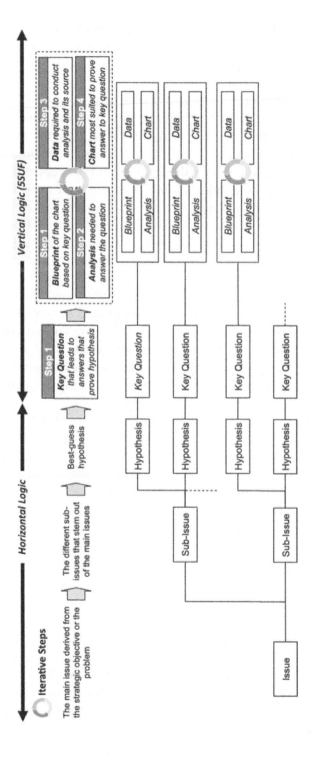

The basic idea here is to take a big issue or problem and break it down into possible root causes based on your hypothesis. It is therefore a process that leads to you asking the right questions.

When you come up with a hypothesis, you need to know that it is actually feasible. This means that the idea that "anything can happen," while generally true, is not very useful for STC or for the purpose of formalizing hypotheses. Given that, a hypothesis that you come up with has to be specific and quality driven. It cannot be vague or generalized. An excellent way of checking whether or not your hypothesis fits this definition is to run a litmus test to see whether you can develop an argument that can disprove your hypothesis. If you can come up with such an argument, then that will mean you need to further revise or solidify your hypothesis before moving to the next phase of the process.

When a strategy consultant is hired, the first thing they will do is to identify what the right questions to ask their client are. They will take care to do this as quickly as they possibly can. To that end, they will develop questionnaires which they will then use to interview client staff. The answers they get during these interview sessions will help them reinforce and expand on their hypotheses and issue diagrams.

As you may recall, the issue diagram makes use of vertical logic for each hypothesis. Once a consultant has established what the right questions to ask are, they will need to phrase every hypothesis and claim a headline. It's at this point that a hypothesis will begin transforming into a headline or claim that charts will go on to prove. Once headlines are written, all that the consultant will have to do will be to organize them in a storyline that flows using punchier phrases. That means they'll have to ensure that each headline is as impactful and memorable as possible, the same way that the punchline of a joke would be.

Structured Thinking Hacks

Like I said before, the most valuable skill I learned as a strategy consultant is structured thinking. The first step to using your structured thinking skills is to make use of the issue diagram. But your horizontal logic will only be complete when you are able to articulate your entire story through solid, flowing, and punchy headlines. In other words, your work won't be complete until you start organizing your content and actually putting them into a structure.

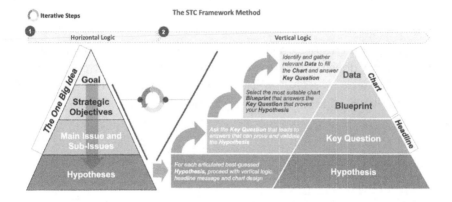

The first step to organizing your work is to start out with a goal in mind. Then you move on to figuring out your strategic objectives to the best of your abilities. You can go about revising them while you develop your charts and go through the process of proving your hypotheses one-by-one. While you're at it, you can periodically update your strategic objectives and resolve your issue diagram until you feel that your strategic objectives have, at last, become solid and crystallized.

To sum up, the way to achieve this is to develop a deck blueprint and storyline structure, run through your headlines and apply the litmus test. You can conduct a litmus test by asking two questions:

- What is the one main takeaway from my storyline?
- Did the main takeaway achieve my goal?

Remember, your strategic objectives and how you drive the story flow may differ. Your strategic objectives are what you need to have in place to take your audience on a journey that will achieve your goal. They define your narrative and the flow of your storyline.

The "So What" Factor

There's a question you need to ask yourself every time you finish making a chart: So what? If what that chart is telling you does not link back to your strategic objectives and goals, then it needs to be removed from the deck. Alternatively, it can be revised until the answer to that question—so what?—starts directly or indirectly reinforcing your big idea.

Every time you complete a chart, ask the question at the end: So What? If the answer does not link to your strategic objectives or goal, remove it from the deck or revise until you have an answer to that "so what?" that directly or indirectly reinforces the big idea.

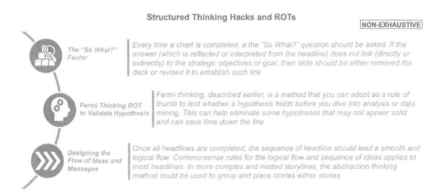

Structured Thinking Hacks and ROTs

NON-EXHAUSTIVE

The "So What?" Factor — Every time a chart is completed, a the "So What?" question should be asked. If the answer (which is reflected or interpreted from the headline) does not link (directly or indirectly) to the strategic objectives or goal, then slide should be either removed the deck or revised it to establish such link

Fermi Thinking ROT to Validate Hypothesis — Fermi thinking, described earlier, is a method that you can adopt as a rule of thumb to test whether a hypothesis holds before you dive into analysis or data mining. This can help eliminate some hypotheses that may not appear solid and can save time down the line

Designing the Flow of Ideas and Messages — Once all headlines are completed, the sequence of headline should lead a smooth and logical flow. Commonsense rules for the logical flow and sequence of ideas applies to most headlines. In more complex and nested storylines, the abstraction thinking method could be used to group and place stories within stories

Fermi Thinking

Fermi thinking, which was described earlier in VL, is one method you can adopt as a rule of thumb for the horizontal logic as you design your issue diagram. It can be used to test whether a hypothesis holds before you dive into analysis or data mining. This can help you eliminate some hypotheses that may not be as solid as they need to be. As such, Fermi thinking can save you a lot of time down the line.

Design the Flow of Ideas and Messages

Once you have put all the headlines together, you'll be ready to take the final step in HL, which is to structure the flow of your headlines, so that they run smoothly and logically. To that end, there are some common sense rules that you can follow. These rules can help you design your sequence automatically, at least in most of your slides.

The most important common sense rule you should keep in mind is that you shouldn't repeat information. What you want to do instead is to introduce unbacked claims early in your story, so that you can go on to prove them later. Claims follow a natural sequence in that some can be used to back others. Considering that, it's important that you start your story with the charts that will back your claims.

Another common sense method you can use to structure your flow, particularly when dealing with longer decks and stories, is to design a hierarchy of ideas. These ideas will cascade upwards from individual stories or slides toward the big idea. Similarly, they will cascade down from the big idea to the individual stories or slides so that they can be supported.

The Abstract Thinking Method

The abstract thinking method is my go-to method for structuring decks. Though I'm now able to do this intuitively, putting my thoughts down on paper at the beginning of each project and visualizing abstractions in a graph like mindmaps is a technique that still helps me. This is also a good tool for me to help structure and divide up the work I need to do when I'm working with team members.

Before I dive into how abstract thinking works, let's first grasp the concept. If you have a simple storyline or what I consider to be a simple linear problem or issue, you can typically resolve it using an equally simple tree structure. This structure should be a single-issue tree. That way, structuring your story will be as easy as following the sequence. Of course, real life seldom tends to be that easy. So, we need to heed Einstein's words and "make everything as simple as possible, but not simpler."

Most real-life business problems consist of interrelated multi-level issues. When you put those issues into a diagram, they tend to differ in levels of abstraction. That means that you can break down a single issue into multiple different ones and assign each one a hypothesis. Conversely, an issue might be a standalone one but could lead to different hypotheses. You may even have different issues that link to the same hypothesis.

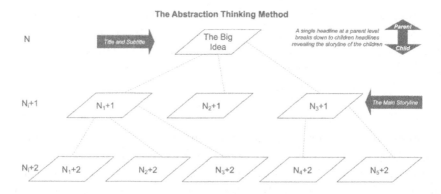

The Abstraction Thinking Method

Think about it this way: If you were to take all your charts, of which you may have 50 or more, and tried to make a story with them, your brain would find managing their order and organizing them into a story to be a challenge. This is where abstraction and hierarchy both come into play and help you to organize everything. Worry not, an excellent tool to visually manage these hierarchies will be described later under mind maps.

For now, let's focus more on abstraction, which is a concept that's often used in system thinking. In system thinking the most basic level of a system is called elements (Benoît Mandelbrot, 2006). In our case, the elements in question are the individual headlines and charts we have.

Abstraction removes successive levels of detail from a presentation to capture only the essential features of a system in a specific layer, as the blueprints of physical structures do. Through the process of abstraction, a building designer can hide or show irrelevant insights about the whole structure they're working on to reduce its complexity and become able to focus only on its essence.

As the name implies, hierarchy lets you define how much the audience is exposed to at any given point in time. It also organizes the chunks of content exposure that the audience experiences. This makes it possible for the brain to digest what it's being given in a logical and deliberate sequence.

Let's now examine how this works in the context of STC, when structuring horizontal logic and the flow of your storyline. As I described earlier, some of your issues are, in fact, sub-issues that lead to hypotheses and charts. These hypotheses and charts are, again, the elements of the systems.

When you're applying abstract thinking to STC, you're leveraging the concept of layering the issues and sub-issues according to their level from N to Ni+X, with "X" representing the maximum number of levels in a story, and "i" representing the number of issues that exist at that particular level.

Once you have all the levels and their hierarchies laid out, then you can structure your storyline in this way. For clarification, the levels below others are referred to as "children" and the levels above others are referred to as "parents" here:

Each level is considered to be one single story, but your main story is the headlines at level N+1. N+1 is made up of Ni+1, where "i" is the number of headlines found at level N+1.

As you see from the hierarchy, Ni+1 can have children on its own. What's more, some of its children at level Ni+2 can have children at level Ni+3 and so on and so forth. For the sake of simplicity, let's assume N+2 is the deepest level of your hierarchy. If this is the case, you can use this example to illustrate the hierarchy of your story:

N1+1; N1+2; N2+2; N3+2; N2+1; N3+1; N4+2; N5+2

Ultimately, how your story reads will determine the exact flow it takes. That flow must make logical sense and this hierarchy will establish the initial blueprint for that to be the case.

To picture this, think of these relationships like movie plots with several characters, each of whom have their own story. All of these stories will eventually come together and intersect with the main plot. Before then, though, you would have to structure a storyboard of the movie, so that you can keep the plot and individual stories moving forward, without confusing your audience and giving away the ending, while keeping them engaged.

Put simply, then, you need to structure your story so that it has multiple layers. Those layers should cascade up to your main message and big idea. In the end, you will use copy boarding to stitch all those messages and headlines together, as will be discussed later. This will turn your HL into the glue that holds your VL together in a logical and engaging flow.

Other Popular and Supplemental Methods

The good news about STC is that it doesn't require you to purchase any kind of software. Still, having software tools at hand to visualize and structure abstract layers and the issue diagram, like mind mapping tools, can be very useful. Such tools will only briefly be discussed here though, as there is plenty of other content to plow through, such as the Pyramid Principle.

The Minto Pyramid Principle

Invented by Barbara Minto, this was McKinsey's attempt to standardize STC training for newcomers. Minto later popularized the principle in her international best-selling book of the same name (Minto, 1987).

Minto's framework, first published in book format in the 1980s, is the only published work written by a senior consultant who practiced strategy consulting at McKinsey for a decade to exist on the market today. In fact, Minto herself was the first female MBA hire at McKinsey and worked in strategy consulting when the field was still evolving.

Barbara has said, "It was, in fact, a golden time to be at McKinsey, an exciting time to be in consulting because there was a lot of thinking about structure. We were inventing all the major analytical frameworks still in use today...." (Minto, 2010)

Her method is based on her trademarked SCQ Framework (Situation, Complication, Question Framework). The book itself may be too technical for some as its target audience is practicing strategy consultants. That's why I don't believe the method can be adopted as a practical, quick-learning tool by most people. Nonetheless, I recommend purchasing a copy of it or looking up a basic summary of it. This way the book can be a supplemental companion to the STC Framework. You can also learn the SCQ method at your own pace, as it is not a prerequisite to the STC framework.

Going back to the actual concept, the Pyramid Principle is somewhat similar to the issue diagram in that it is based on a pyramid structure. This structure cascades down from a single, top-level thought. Below that top-level thought sit your arguments, and those sit your supporting data.

The concept is based on a fixed structure for the sake of the flow of the deck or the story. While this may be appealing to some people, I don't encourage adopting this approach alone, as it only provides one perspective for tackling storylines.

One significant issue I've experienced with apprentices who had studied Minto's method before and tried adopting it is that it resulted in their thinking in a way that was a bit too linear. This, in turn, caused their analysis to become less holistic overall. became less holistic in their analysis.

While the SCQ method works well for the purposes of structuring your storyline, it can ultimately direct you toward linear thinking. This may cause your analysis to become less comprehensive than it otherwise could have been. As a result, you may end up missing the forest for the trees. As an example, one thing you'll end up missing when your thinking becomes too linear is the ability to see how claims might be interdependent. Losing this ability might unfortunately weaken your entire story deck. Considering all this, you could use the Pyramid Principle as an STC supplement, but you should refrain from making it into a substitute for it.

The Modular Presentation Design

Modular design is a design pattern that divides one big system into smaller elements and components that can be put together to recreate that system or combined in unique ways to create new systems (UNext Editorial Team, 2022). These smaller elements and components are typically referred to as modules. These modules can be independently created, easily configured, and even reconfigured into different systems.

When designing a system, you have to decide whether you are going to build a homogenous system—meaning one that can't be split into smaller components—or a modular one. If you were to build a house by pouring out concrete in one continuous go to create unified slaps that would make up that house's joined walls, you would be building a homogenous structure. If, on the other hand, you were to construct that house out of bricks stacked atop one another and glued together using cement, you would certainly be creating a modular structure.

As you might guess from that example, modularity is a popular feature often found in complex engineering systems, which are made up of all sorts of different wires, knobs, buttons, levers, and more. Given how complex modular systems can be, dividing homogeneous systems into separate components is actually much easier to do than trying to put those modules back together to create a bigger system.

So, why does all this matter? Now that we understand what a modular system is, how can we design one in STC? To do this we will need three different things: a module, an interface, and a set of protocols that are connected to those modules. To create a module we will first need to unbundle the monolithic system we have. In computer science, this technique is called the separation of concerns because it means turning each component into a separate, that is to say, autonomous concern. Countries you would see when looking at a world map, for example, would be separate concerns, seeing as they each have autonomy but are also components making up the world.

The way we go about dividing a system into modules is incredibly important. We cannot just do this by drawing arbitrary lines without properly inspecting the systems that lie behind them. If we try, we are sure to encounter many problems later on. A module is meant to both define distinct, separate functions and also encapsulate them. It is therefore something that can make internal mechanics into abstracts separate from the larger system. The process of doing this is known as black–boxing.

In science and engineering, a block box is a device or system that can be viewed in terms of its output, input, and transfer characteristics, without its internal workings being taken into consideration. These inputs, outputs, and characteristics are defined using an interface that can tell other modules in a system what those separate elements will do. You can liken this to your LinkedIn profile. Your profile is basically an interface telling others what you do. At the same time, this interface tells them what people might expect to receive if they give them something. It tells a potential employer looking at your profile what services you'll give them if they give you a new job.

When working on a modular design, we need to find some way of joining all those modules or separate concerns. In other words, we need a way to couple them. This coupling may be loose, meaning that modules might retain a certain degree of autonomy after they're put together. Alternatively, the coupling might be tight, meaning that the modules would lose their autonomy and become constrained in their interactions with the system, as well as with the other modules. To succeed at coupling modules, you need to establish a set of protocols to define what terms, agreements, and common language your modules will need to operate and interact with one another.

The advantageous thing about modular presentation design is that it can make distributed collaboration and problem-solving a whole lot easier. By breaking your story into different components, you can simplify a very complex problem or system. In doing so, you can tackle them one-by-one, then put them together in a logical flow that makes it possible for your audience to understand the larger story in all its details. You can also distribute the modules among your team members and have them work on them. This is by far the best advantage this design has to offer. However, you must do this without losing sight of the interdependencies among them. Large or complex presentations or systems are nonlinear systems that should be tackled holistically and not in a reductionist manner.

Mind Mapping

Mind mapping is the simplest of all possible methods yet it's one you don't often see in strategy consulting training. This method relies on using spider-shaped maps that illustrate a hierarchical, radiant structure. It's designed to allow you to visualize complex concepts and make it easy for your brain to digest them. These maps can then turn complex ideas into hierarchies and help you visualize a full storyline deck, as well as headlines in abstract layers.

Mind mapping can reflect the issue diagram showing the actual problem and help you to set up and test your slides' sequences using a software presentation feature.

Mindmap Example

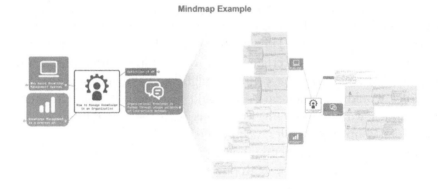

Mind mapping can also help you pick up the pace when you're building a mock-up and designing the blueprint of your story and horizontal logic, before you ever dive into the details of the vertical logic.

Given all these benefits, the fact that consultants don't use mind mapping more often is baffling to me. Personally, I find it to be a super useful tool to build blueprinting storylines. There are plenty of software tools out there that can help you build mind maps, so I advise you to add this to your arsenal.

Storyboarding and Copy Boarding

You're probably familiar with storyboarding. It's a term generally used by film producers when they're designing their structures. It's also used by creatives when they're mapping out scenes in movies, TV show episodes, and even commercials. I adopt storyboarding in three ways: I alternate between electronic apps, sticky notes, and A4 or a letter-sized sheet of blank paper.

Some people find structuring their thoughts offline on colored sticky pads to be useful. I prefer sticking with a pen and paper, especially when I'm still in the design and brainstorming stage. I usually combine that with copy boarding, where I use sticky pads to design the flow of the headlines. Then I have a team member put all of that into a mind map and assign a team leader for each story within the story.

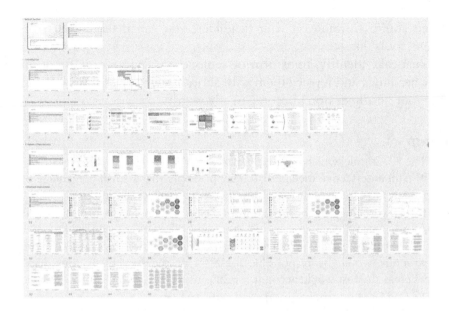

How to Draft Headlines

There are a couple of rules you should abide by when you're working on your headlines. These are:

- **Be specific, not generic**. Remember that your headline needs to convey what the slide it's in is going to be talking about. It needs to give your audience an idea about your message the instant that they look at it and this can only be achieved through specificity.

- **Focus on outcomes**. Focusing on outcomes in headlines will set your audience's expectation on what to expect and pique their curiosity a little about how that outcome was arrived at. As such, it will increase audience engagement.

- **Quantify insights.** The old "numbers speak louder than words" rule applies here as well, curiously enough. Numbers are generally irrefutable, so by quantifying your insights in headlines, you'll be presenting your audience with solid facts immediately. You'll, again, be setting their expectations and increasing their engagement.

- **Use short sentences.** As a general rule, always stick with short sentences and one-liners if you can. Whatever you do, do not let your headlines exceed two lines. The human attention span is fairly short, as you'll remember. So, if you keep headlines long, your audience's attention will wander and you will lose engagement.

When you're working on your headlines, you can make use of free, online tools like Steve Hanov's Zinsser transformer. Such tools automatically identify, transform or remove common words found in your headlines and replace them with shorter alternatives. This ensures that your headlines don't become overly wordy.

Recap

- The 80/20 rule, which is a kind of power law, isn't always exact. Regardless it's still an effective metaphor for the principle that a small percentage of something can account for a larger percentage of something else.
- If you were to apply the 80/20 rule to scale, you could say that you would spend 20% of your time on structure and 80% of it on things like data analysis and working on individual charts. Of these two things, though, the structure would be responsible for 80% of the success of your deck, whereas the rest would account for 20% of it.
- To build a good structure and convey the right messages in your story, you need to start the process by crystallizing your strategic objectives.
- Like universal goals, you'll need to articulate each and every one of your strategic objectives separately.
- You can solve any problem, so long as you ask the right questions about it.
- The issue diagram has you take a big issue or problem and break it down into possible root causes based on your hypothesis. It is therefore a process that leads to you asking the right questions.
- Every time you complete a chart, ask the question at the end: So What?
- Fermi thinking can be used to test whether a hypothesis holds before you dive into analysis or data mining.
- Ultimately, how your story reads will determine the exact flow it takes. That flow must make logical sense and this hierarchy will establish the initial blueprint for that to be the case.
- The SCQ method works well for the purposes of structuring your storyline, it can ultimately direct you toward linear thinking. This may cause your analysis to become less comprehensive than it otherwise could have been.
- The modular design is a design pattern built around the idea that any given system can be divided into smaller components known as modules.
- Mind mapping is the simplest of all possible methods and can reflect the issue diagram showing the actual problem and help you to set up and test your slides' sequences using a software presentation feature.
- When drafting headlines be specific, focus on outcomes, quantify insights, and use short sentences.

Chapter 5: Storytelling Hacks

Copy is not written. Copy is assembled. –Eugene Schwartz

In this chapter, we'll explore various storytelling techniques and hacks that you can make use of in your presentations, which I refer to as STC hacks. These hacks can be used to improve and enhance your stories. While they can be nice to have, they are not replacements for the core STC framework. With that in mind, and before we dive into the hacks, you should know that there are two things that can be detrimental to your story if they occur in your storyline. These are things you want to avoid at all costs. If these instances occur, no hack or technique can help which is why they should not occur at all.

In 1995, OJ Simpson's murder trial was all over the news. At the time, OJ was on trial for the murder of his wife, Nicole Brown Simpson, and her friend Ron Goldman. One of the trial's most surprising moments occurred when assistant prosecutor Christopher Darden asked OJ to try on a bloodstained glove that had been found on the scene. He believed that the glove had been worn during the murder and that it would fit OJ's hand. Putting on the glove was, very clearly a struggle, though, as can be seen in the video footage available of the scene. OJ tried to push his hand into it several times and kept grimacing in pain and complaining that it was too tight all the while (Campbell, 2020).

Since Daren had already indicated that the glove had been worn during the murder, by the murderer, the fact that it didn't fit OJ's hand was incredibly problematic for him. Instead of demonstrating that OJ was the murderer, the incident cast doubt on the prosecutor's case. It raised the possibility that there was another murderer, another culprit responsible for the crime, at least in the jury's mind. Put simply, it proved Rozin's "single drop of sewage" theory, in that one small piece of incorrect evidence killed the entire case that the prosecutor was building against OJ. So the lesson here is that you want to avoid mistakes at all costs, along with errors, unsubstantiated claims, or anything that can discredit you, your story, or your case, thereby triggering suspicions in your audience's mind. Even if you did everything right to that point, all it takes is one such mishap, and your entire story "goes to sh*t"

The second important thing to watch for is your first impression. You've probably heard the saying "first impressions matter." Whether you are presenting in person or writing an intro of a deck, the first few slides or a couple of slides create the first impression for your audience or reader. While I'll get into related hacks in this chapter, but if you don't want to hack the intro, by all means, don't mess it up. Once a first impression has been formed, reversing it becomes exceedingly difficult. Hence, setting a good first impression for your audience is incredibly important in STC. It's something that affects how willing they will be to listen to and believe you. It's something that'll impact how persuasive you will be in your pitch. It's even something that will even play a part in how willing they will be to listen to you in the first place.

Now that we got that out of the way, let's dive into storytelling hacks.

The Universal Structure

If you want to set the right first impression and articulate your ideas effectively, one ROT you need to call to mind is that you need to keep your "ask" to a minimum in STC STC, no matter what your purpose, goal or strategic objectives are. The primary structure you need to adopt is the 80/20 principle, which can be applied to all subject matters. Remember that 80% of the content you will present in your study will be based on the 3DF. More or less 20% of it, meanwhile, will be dedicated to what actions you want your audience to take or what you expect from your audience, regardless of STC.

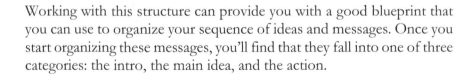

You need to keep your "ask" to a minimum in STC, no matter what your purpose, goal or strategic objectives are.

Working with this structure can provide you with a good blueprint that you can use to organize your sequence of ideas and messages. Once you start organizing these messages, you'll find that they fall into one of three categories: the intro, the main idea, and the action.

How you begin your story, that is to say how you give a first impression, is just as overlooked an element of storytelling as it is important. The way you begin a story is sometimes called the lead potion, but for the purposes of this book, we'll refer to it as the intro. The intro is the part of the story that puts the storyline into context. It's what sets the stage for what's to come.

So, why is that important? You've likely heard the intro be talked about in many ways. The elevator pitch, the handshake… Your intro is your chance to set an impression on your audience when you're meeting them for the first time. Often we form impressions of other people even before they get a chance to speak. In fact, we set our first impression of people approximately five to 30 seconds into meeting them. How quickly we form that impression depends on the context that we're meeting them in (Irmak Olcaysoy Okten, 2018). Telling a story or making a presentation to people is no exception to this. When you're making a presentation, there's no doubt that your audience will pass some kind of judgment on you, be it a positive or negative one. Seeing as the information age has shortened everyone's attention span, they'll be very quick to do so, too. This means that you, as the presenter, are under a fair bit of pressure to capture your audience's attention moments into meeting them. You need to be intriguing enough to hook your audience as soon as you begin your presentation or even walk into the room. Doing so is the only way to hook them and keep them engaged. This is the main reason why the title and subtitle of your presentation are so vital. It's as David Oglivy says in his book *The Confessions of an Advertising Man*: headlines are truly the most important in advertising and play a determining role in whether the audience will pay attention to an ad. The same logic easily applies to your headlines, and a good headline can get your audience to start reading your intro at the very least.

What you want to do with your intro is to generate enough emotions and trigger sufficient interest on the part of the audience to make them crave more. You want to use your intro as a hook to make them want to know more. By using your intro, you want to make them feel that they'll be getting exactly what they want and need in the rest of the presentation. If you can accomplish that, you will easily be able to capture their attention. Naturally, the first step to pulling off this impossible-sounding feat is to create a truly captivating title.

Remember: the main takeaway here is that your intro sets the pace for what's to come, as well as your audience's expectations. As such, it's a key, determining factor in whether or not your audience will keep their attention fixed on your presentation—if it's an in-person one—or keep reading it—if it's not done in person.

"The Big Idea" or "The Core Concept" and a Captivating Title

So, what's the big idea? Contrary to how you're probably hearing that question in your mind, the big idea isn't exactly what you think it is. It's not a term that has been invented by the Three Stooges or Bugs Bunny for that matter, especially since it's not followed by the word "doc." Instead, the big idea is your single, most important attention grabber. It may even be the most important characteristic of your story.

The big idea is the one common thread that will be running through all of the individual messages you'll be giving throughout your story. It will form the spine of that story and thereby hold all your individual charts together. Your big idea, then, is what you will use to stitch your charts together to form a meaningful and captivating story.

According to David Ogilvy, the advertising tycoon, the core concept that makes advertising great is placing a single, powerful idea at its center. Ogilvy referred to this idea as the Big Idea. He believed that an ad without a big idea is as ineffective as a ship passing by a shore at the dead of night (Ogilvy, 2013).

Once you figure out what your "big idea" is, you can put it through a litmus test to see if it holds up, much in the way you would do to your hypothesis. This would be a doubly good idea seeing as your hypothesis and your big idea will be intimately connected anyway.

Todd Brown, the creator and the author of the book *E5 Method,* summarizes the big idea using a simple formula that he explains in his books. According to this formula, the big idea has to be both intellectually interesting and emotionally compelling. In other words, it has to appeal both to your audience's logical side and make your emotional side kick into gear. This way it can engage with both System 1 and System 2 in your audience's brains. At the same time, it has to address an urgent problem—ideally the problem your audience is turning to you to solve—and offer a big promise, which should be the solution that you have come up with and are ultimately presenting to your audience. On top of all that, your big idea needs to be unique. In other words, it cannot be something generic that could have been found elsewhere.

Another important influence factor to consider is the first impression. A bad first impression is one of the worst things that can happen to you during a presentation or deck storyline. I recall this one time when I was evaluating one of three research firms that were shortlisted for conducting a large quantitative survey (a contract worth seven figures) for a client and was meeting its rep for the first time. The rep showed up five minutes late and had his ear glued to his phone as he shook my hand. How do you imagine the rest of that meeting went? Studies show that first impressions can be formed in about a second (Wargo, 2006). Within the context of STC, first impressions can be formed in just a few minutes, as you'll discover later on. Given that, it's important that your title, headlines, and intro are dressed to impress, so to speak. A common mistake many people make in this regard is starting off with a boring agenda on their very first slide and presenting it in person. If this is your initial inclination ask yourself: is that agenda really how you want your audience to get their first impression?

Five-Step Approach to Developing the Big Idea

The question then is, how do you develop your big idea and core concept, and make sure that it meets all of these requirements? To accomplish this, you need to adopt a specific approach. Otherwise, it would be hard to expect anyone to come up with a big idea. Luckily, there are several approaches you can take when you're trying to find yours.

Working Backwards

A metaphor for working backward might be the magic wand, because it works as well as actual magic. It's so named because it asks the question "If you could wave your magic wand and give your prospects anything, what would you give?" This technique then has you work backward from the answer you come up with.

Let's say you came up with an idea but aren't sure if it's a good one. There are certain criteria you could use if you want to see whether or not this is the case. These criteria are:

- Is your core concept divergent? In other words, does it differ from what your audience already knows or is aware of?
- Is the content you're providing your audience with specific? Specificity is key to creating interesting, easy-to-grasp solutions and messages that your audience can pick up with cognitive ease. Remember: the more specific your idea is, the more understandable and easy to implement it will be for your audience, which will make it more appealing for them.Is the content, story, or reward you're offering your audience desirable? Is it more desirable than the obstacles they may have to overcome when implementing the idea you're presenting them with? Your content and reward need to be desirable in one way or another if it is going to be picked up by your audience. This is especially true in cases where your idea requires your audience to give something up or change something. Your idea should bring your client a benefit that will outweigh the cost they'll have to pay to get it. It should be "worth it" for your audience to make that idea into their reality. Remember: you'll have to know exactly what your audience wants and what kinds of rewards will be "worth it" for them, if you want to be able to offer them the right content, story, or reward.

You might be wondering what the audience is giving up by listening to you. The short answer to that question is "PLENTY." In the short term, they are giving up their time and attention. These days, people's time/attention come with a heavy price. Everyone's competing for people's attention, and our attention span has shrunk so much that it's equivalent to that of a goldfish. When you are presenting, then, your audience is giving up a very valuable, limited resource. For that to be worth it, you need to give them something that is far more valuable in return if you want to get and retain their attention.

More than anything else, though, nothing beats the power of a compelling story. If you want to present your audience with a good concept, then you need to deliver it in a compelling story. A compelling idea is, as we have seen, one that sparks and triggers certain emotions in your audience. A big idea that is part of such a story is both emotionally compelling and makes a primary promise. A big idea that is emotionally compelling delivers this primary promise—meaning your solution and reward—through a unique mechanism that triggers the emotions you want. Fr example, the big promise can be:

- Be big and bold enough to be memorable, so that it remains fixed in your audience's mind when they walk away from your presentation.
- Make the audience lust after the payoff that you are offering, enough to face potential obstacles when implementing whatever change you're asking them to make.
- Embody the result you are seeking to achieve, which is what your audience will have tasked you to do.
- Be backed by plenty of qualitative and some quantitative proof.
- Solve an urgent problem that your audience either has asked you to solve or that you have identified at their request.
- Make the audience believe and feel "This is exactly what I've been waiting for" because it either answers their questions or presents them with a way to make a problem they've been dealing with go away.

Whatever tactics, strategies, and techniques you offer your audience in your presentation as part of your big idea, the point is that it has to be intellectually interesting while emotionally stimulating if it is to be effective. But what kinds of feelings is the big idea supposed to generate anyways? Well, there are four emotions you want to trigger in your audience. For example, such triggers could be:

- The "wow, this is big" feeling, which can open up your audience's mind and perspective, increase their engagement, and make them more supportive of the ideas that you present.
- A feeling of discovery, where the audience feels they are getting access to something they never knew or considered before, which can make them feel special—the way an explorer might—and accomplished.
- Curiosity, which is a driving factor in any good story, and which can make your audience stick with you throughout the entirety of your presentation and pay close attention to the messages you're giving.

It's a good idea to try to have your big idea and story for that to generate the first three of these feelings because they're all emotions that add value to what you're saying. They give the audience the sense and understanding that you are offering them something they want and need. They also give them the understanding that they're offering them something they couldn't have been able to find anywhere else. The big idea and the story also have to generate curiosity in the audience because curiosity will increase audience engagement. Your audience feeling curious is what will pique their interest and keep it on you and your story throughout your presentation.

A big idea cannot evoke such feelings if the story it's being conveyed to the audience relies solely on logic. The story and the idea need to rely on and utilize emotional devices as well. The best emotional and, frankly speaking, narrative device they can use is metaphors, as you'll see later.

Developing BIG IDEAS

Now that you know all about what a big idea is supposed to look like, it's time to move onto the crux of the matter: how do you develop a big idea? To develop a big idea you need to start brainstorming and generate as many ideas as you possibly can. At this stage, you need not worry about whether an idea is feasible or dumb. Even if it's not, the act of coming up with it and writing it down is important. After all, that "dumb" idea might later spark another idea in your mind and that might turn into your big idea.

If you want to be creative and develop a captivating Big Idea, you have to start by generating lots of possible ideas. To generate a lot of ideas you need to feed off of a lot of sources, even ones that seemingly aren't connected to the field you're trying to generate an idea for. This way, you can draw knowledge and inspiration from a variety of different avenues, combine them in unique ways and come up with a great idea, as well as an effective solution to the problem you're trying to solve. The different sources you can get input from are diverse magazines, news, movies, books, products, interviews, brainstorming sessions with your team, research into what the competition is doing, and more.

The thing about creative ideas is that they're all about looking for new and unusual combinations and connections. You never know where the next big idea is going to come from, so you have to look into every nook and cranny and think outside the box, as they say. The trick isn't to find an odd idea, though. It's to find one that you actually believe in, are excited about, and want to share with others. Those are the real metrics that you need to gauge an idea by. If what you think is a big idea doesn't excite you or if you don't really believe in it, then you either need to lay it to rest or you haven't evolved it into its final form. If you find that you're struggling to come up with ideas—experiencing a writer's block of the mind, so to speak—you could try using an artificial intelligence (AI) idea generator. By now, you've probably heard of how amazing AI has gotten to be in doing all sorts of things from writing poems and short stories to creating digital works of art. It shouldn't surprise you, then, that AI idea generators have gotten just as good. You don't have to use ideas that you come up with using an AI generator, of course. But the ones that you get from it can be a great starting point for you and, at the very least, kick your brainstorming and creative thinking skills into action.

Your ability to generate a new idea from all of these different sources depends on two things: your creativity and your capacity to combine old, familiar elements in ways that allow you to see new relationships. In creating your idea, you can imagine that your audience is divided into two groups: rentiers and speculators. Rentiers are those individuals who see different elements as entirely separate and disconnected from one another. Speculators, on the other hand, see that different elements are in fact connected, even if they come from seemingly opposite fields like art and neuroscience. Speculators are those individuals who can see these connections and combine separate elements. They see these elements as links in the grand chain of knowledge. Needless to say, when you're trying to think of your big idea in STC, you want to be a speculator, as opposed to a rentier.

When you're trying to find your bid idea, then, you have to look for relationships between things that you ordinarily wouldn't think are connected. You also absolutely shouldn't wait around for inspiration to strike. Contrary to popular belief, inspiration isn't something that will suddenly come to you when you're sitting in your office, lazing about. It's something you have to look for constantly, by sifting through copious amounts of information.

There are two types of information you'll have to sift through in this process: specific information and general information. Specific information will be data that's related to a particular situation, case, or problem that you have been investigating, questioning, or discussing in your proposal. General information, on the other hand, will be more general information that you have access to about, say, the market or industry your audience is in. You can make use of both these data sets in your presentations. Using specific information in STC, for instance, can help you to question how your audience or client achieved the success they already have. Once you uncover the minutiae of your audience's beliefs, aims, and goals, you can incorporate them into your presentation and use them to develop and support your main idea. You can then combine this specific information with more general concepts, like ones pertaining to behavioral science, for instance, the way I have been doing throughout this book.

Of course, there are several strategies you need to keep in mind as you go about developing your big idea. These rules will stop you from limiting or constricting yourself:

- Strategy #1: Come up with as many ideas as you possibly can. Do not judge any of your ideas and label them as "stupid" or anything of the sort. If you're feeling stuck, use an AI idea generator to come up with new things and keep brainstorming.
- Strategy #2: Note the key proof points of all the ideas you come up with, as in literally writing them down. This will help you later. Make sure that those proof points are both emotionally and intellectually appealing.
- Strategy #3: Remember that you are not writing content. This is simply developing the big idea, so you don't have to worry about being too verbose or anything like that (yet).
- Strategy #4: Ask yourself questions about your idea such as…
- Why would other people be interested in this idea?
- Why would they care?
- How does this idea impact this audience?
- Strategy #5: Give yourself ample time to actually think on, research, and develop your big idea.
- Strategy #6: Don't start expanding on your big idea until you feel the need to do so and you feel ready to do so. If you feel that you don't yet have enough information to be able to follow the concept through, then you likely don't.
- Strategy #7: Do a test elevator pitch of your idea. This pitch should summarize your big idea in a concise—no more than two sentences long—and clear statement and express it powerfully but simply.

To summarize then, the process of coming up with a big idea starts with the research. You then move on to looking for connections between the different elements you've identified and organizing your notes. Once you're done with that, you'll have started coming up with ideas. It's important that you write down your ideas as you come up with them, lest you forget. Finally, once you have written your ideas and chosen the one(s) you want, you start revising and polishing it until you can express it the way you want.

Now that you have your big idea, though, you'll need to craft a title that can accurately and quickly capture it. That title will then drive the structure of your introduction section. You can consider crafting your title an experiment of sorts. Start by writing down a long list of possible titles and then shorten that list through a process of elimination. Once you have your short list, run it by a close circle of friends to see which one works best.

The Intro

The intro is the first two to five minutes of your story, which translates to your initial two to five slides or charts, depending on how complicated your intro and story are. It is how your audience will first cast judgment on what you have to say and what will set the stage for engagement. Once these initial five minutes have passed, you will have missed your chance to make an impression. As such, you need to make excellent use of them when you can.

Once you've established your big idea, your next step will be to expand on it and start thinking about how you want to maintain engagement. It's important that you do this, because while those first moments might win your audience's attention, you will need to hold onto it as your story goes on.

Your right intro and title basically account for about 4% of your story. Yet they will account for 64% of its success. That right there is the 80/20 of the 80/20 of your story.

There are many types of intros you can use to ensure that you catch your audience's attention from the get-go. Here are some general examples from intros that I frequently use in my story deck intros:

- The cased based intros, which are story-led and can be used if you have a strong, interesting story in your hands that will immediately catch your audience's attention.
- The shocking statement-based intro, which, as per its name, delivers a shocking, though not untrue, statement to get the audience interested.

- The ultimate benefit or value-based intro or the promise, which lays out the benefits that the audience will get from the story, thereby creating a sense of anticipation gets them interested.
- The strategy intro, which lays out your proposed strategy without giving away too much to create a sense of curiosity and a desire to know more

Identifying Beliefs and Objections

As discussed earlier, in the chapter about beliefs, the reason you probably want to understand our audience's beliefs is because you want to identify the possible objections that our claim or story might face. You want to establish these objections early on, so that you can tackle them head-on with your claims and proofs. You might not think of this process as building your story. However, just because something isn't an obvious fact to you, doesn't mean it isn't an obvious fact to your audience.

This is why, when selecting jurors for a court of law, for example, both the prosecution and the lawyers prepare a set of questions they want to ask to the jury candidates. By asking these questions, they ensure that none of the people chosen for the jury have any prior or preconceived beliefs that might make them biased for or against one side or the other. The process of understanding your audience's beliefs follows the same logic. Except, unlike a prosecutor, you don't have the luxury of selecting your audience yourself. Given that, you need to assume that your audience holds the worst beliefs that might set them against your proposals and prepare yourself and your arguments accordingly.

To accomplish this, you'll need to identify universal beliefs, as opposed to specific beliefs. The thing is, you can never nail down what any one individual's beliefs and objections will be. Especially since sometimes a person's beliefs aren't even all that obvious to themselves.

If you want to identify the universal beliefs that concern you and your STC, you need to ask certain questions to identify and understand beliefs that run counter to your own:
- What other experiences might be possible or valid?
- What might you not have noticed?
- What other theories are conceivable?
- What other conclusions might be reached?

- What other beliefs might be valid?

The Executive Summary and the 5 Ideas (5is)

The executive summary refers to your next 5–30 or fewer charts or messages, following your intro. There have been times when I've had to summarize a 500-page deck in a 15-page presentation, which would be used to present my ideas to CEOs or executive committees. This is an often encountered challenge in STC. Personally, I am able to easily synthesize any size deck into 25+ charts or messages. But this reduction and summary task becomes a challenge even for me when the number of charts I have to work with drops to less than 25. At that point, getting all information and the messages I need to convey becomes exceedingly difficult.

This difficulty arises from the fact that you're not dealing with just one, the single idea in a given story. If you have more than five ideas that you need to convey then you're faced with a big problem, because most people won't be able to remember that many ideas. Human memory is limited. A person can remember, at max, five items at a given time (Cowan, 2010). Given that, you need to be able to synthesize all your analysis into, at most, five ideas (5is). As an ROT, remember that 5is is the absolute limit of ideas your audience will be able to remember. If you have more than 5is, then the only way you can keep them in is by making them a subset of one of your others. This way that additional idea might be remembered in relation to one of the original 5is.

As you'll remember, one study has shown that most people can remember an average of 3-4 things at once without turning to any memory aids in the process (Rouder et al., 2011). However, with a bit of enhancement through memory aid techniques in presentation, you can make the mind recall an additional one to two things. That's why, we have our 5i Framework built around 5 ideas. You need to design your story for the average person and assume that you need to focus on 5 things. As such, when writing decks or presentations, an extra effort should be given to a maximum of 5 ideas or takeaways from your story deck.

If you really want to make the messages you're giving in your presentation memorable, though, turning to the memory hacks we've discussed is the way to go. Repetition, for instance, is a very important key to making your ideas memorable for your audience. Hence, this book repeats important facts a couple of different times, in a couple of different ways. But you don't just have to verbally repeat your important messages throughout your presentation. You can also use visual memory cues, which is another memory hack you can employ in your presentations, as you may remember.

What all this means is that you have another ROT to remember which is that the main ideas you present in a deck or story must not be more than five. Ultimately, what you need to focus on is how you can make each of these messages impactful. This is why, the shorter I have to make an executive summary, the more time I spend developing my "Five Ideas" and the support I offer them. To do so, I adopt the same process that I use in identifying the big idea. I create as many big ideas as possible, then lead with five in every presentation.

You need to keep your "ask" to a minimum in STC, no matter what your purpose, goal or strategic objectives are.

Having a good story to tell is important but what makes a story great is the narrative. The narrative is the way to bring your story to life. To craft a good narrative in STC, you need to link the emotional triggers of your story to the professional world and to the story that you're telling. As always, there are several tactics you can use to accomplish this.

The Open Loop and Cliffhanger Method

I'm writing these words while experiencing some violent turbulence on a private jet, which woke me up three hours earlier than I wanted to, during a ten-hour journey on my way to an all-star party and week-long retreat in Mykonos. When I woke up, everyone was holding onto the edge of their seats. I couldn't help but recall the one incident that was the defining moment that changed everything in my life... I'll tell you what happened momentarily, but before I do...

The first thing I do when creating the intro is to open the loop with a big idea. This is because doing this creates a sense of anticipation and uncertainty among the audience. This is a psychological tactic that's often used in dramatic plays, because it can get people instantly engaged with the story they're hearing. The brief story that I just told you is an extreme illustration of the open-loop and cliffhanger method. But more on that later...

Yes, as you can see I just utilized the same tactic that I was describing in the above paragraph. Another example of this in story format might be:

"He suddenly ran out of the apartment, screaming at the top of his lungs. Everyone turned to stare and I took off after him. I saw that his shirt was stained red and that he was hurt. I needed to stop him and get him help immediately, I thought, but I couldn't even begin to guess what had really happened to my friend Mike. Before I share more of his story though, let me put things into some context and explain..."

A story that begins with a cliffhanger usually doesn't end there, of course. The following narrative should have other cliffhangers in it using both open and closed loops in a sequence, illustrated as follows. When you open the big idea loop, though, that loop doesn't close until the very end of the story. When you do get to the end, you'll typically have a series of open loops. You'll then close them, one loop at a time, until you can finally close off the last one, which will belong to your big idea.

If you'll notice, I opened a loop at the beginning of this book but didn't tell you where in the book I'll close it. This is because I know that you couldn't help but skip to the part where I'll close the loop, which is the end of the book. This, however, isn't something that an audience can do in a presentation. You can, however, remind your audience that the loop will be closed at the end, by mentioning it here and there throughout the presentation, thus keeping their sense of anticipation alive.

The Story Arc

To tell a good story, you need to craft a solid story arc that describes the shape of the change you aim to see and its value throughout the entirety of that story. Story arcs have certain points where they either rise or fall. The points they rise, meaning when things get tense and anticipation is built, are high points like climaxes. The points they fall into are the aftermath, where problems are resolved and happy endings are delivered. A story arc, often referred to as a "narrative arc" describes the emotional experience your storyline intends to give your audience. It's what fiction, films, or TV series consider to be the dramatic effect that the plot of your story intends to achieve.

There may be one or many rise and fall-moments in a story arc. This is because stories are essentially a series of events. The fortunes of the stories of characters, which change at those rise and fall moments, interest the audience greatly and can be plotted out in the form of a curved line. When story arcs and characters' fortunes are graphed out like this, seeing the patterns that play out throughout a story becomes possible. Take, for instance, Kurt Vonnegut's *Man in a Hole.*

As you can see, the x-axis of this graph describes the chronology that the story's narrative follows, while the y-axis describes the positive and negative moments of a character's experiences.

Story arcs can be character arcs themselves, illustrating the characters' development as they go through it in the plot. But while all character arcs are story arcs, not all story arcs are character arcs. That means that some story arcs are bound to illustrate things that are separate from the main characters' character development (Bunting, 2020).

Types of Story Arcs

As you might have grasped from the earlier paragraph, there are different kinds of story arcs that you can make use of in your narrative. Though all stories undergo change, not all of them change in the same way. This can be best seen when you look at the graphs of different stories. The more stories you look at, however, the more you realize that specific kinds of stories follow specific types of story arcs.

Story arcs are very important when telling any kind of story—be it in a presentation, a novel, or a movie—because these arcs evoke certain emotions in their audiences. These emotions, such as excitement and curiosity get audiences invested and more willing to absorb the information that those stories are presenting to them. Given that story arcs can also be referred to as emotional arcs, as they make certain kinds of emotions peak at certain points in stories. Stories that use certain different kinds of emotional arcs are more effective in getting their audiences involved when they hit these peaks (Reagan et al., 2016). At least that's what Andrew Reagan and his team of researchers from the University of Vermont found out after analyzing over 4,000 of the best novels from the Project Gutenberg library (Reagan et al., 2016).

Reagan and his team discovered that stories have six kinds of primary arcs. The first of these is the rags-to-riches story. This type of story arc shows a continuous upward climb that ends when the reader gets to the happy ending.

The **rags-to-riches** story arc is the kind of story arc we grow up hearing. As you might have guessed from the name, it's typically found in fairy tales, where the hero starts out with nothing and ends up with everything. They aren't all that popular among "adult" stories though. Still, a number of well-known stories follow this arc, such as Disney's *Tangled* and William Shakespeare's *A Winter's Tale*. The rags to riches story is an uplifting emotional arc with a happy ending. The happy ending obvious generates positive emotions in the audience like relief and the arc of the story generates emotions such as curiosity, which get the audience more invested in the story.

Next up, there's the riches-to-rags arc. This is the kind of story where the hero starts out with everything or almost everything and then proceeds to lose it all. As the story progresses the protagonist's luck keeps getting worse, until their life becomes a shade of their former one. Great examples of this type of arc are J.D. Salinger's *The Catcher in the Rye* and Goethe's *Sorrows of Young Werther*. This kind of arc is an emotional downer, so to speak. As such, it is one you may want to avoid, unless you're painting a picture of what the situation looks like before your Big Idea is implemented.

Then there is the **Man in the Hole** arc, which is a favorite for many storytellers. After all, they have their protagonists experience both good luck and bad luck, rises and falls. In this sense, they tend to be very life-like and realistic. That doesn't mean that the stories that are told with this arc have to be realistic themselves. If that were the case, J.R.R. Tolkien couldn't have written the Lord of the Rings series and Lewis Carrol certainly couldn't have written *Alice in Wonderland*. This kind of emotional arc generates a lot of curiosity "how is this going to end?" or "how will the protagonist get out of this one?" It also generates feelings of relief and happiness with the happy ending, meaning when your Big Idea is presented. As such, it can be a great arc to use for STC.

The same goes for the emotional arc known as **the Double Man in a Whole.** This may well be the most popular arc out of all of them. This type of story has its protagonist experience both bad luck and good luck multiple times and in succession. Luckily, stories that adhere to this format usually end with happy endings, the way J.K. Rowling's *Harry Potter* series does, for instance. Like Man in the Whole, this arc can generate lots of curiosity and ultimately, positive emotions like relief, thereby getting your audience to become really engaged with and invested in the story you're telling.

There is a type of arc that describes first a downturn, then an upturn. This is known as the **Icarus/Freytag's Pyramid** (Freytag, 1863). The arc gets its name after the tragic Greek protagonist, Icarus, who flew too close to the sun despite his father's warning not to do so, burned off his wings, and fell to his death. Don't let the arc name fool you though. These stories don't always have a bad ending, though they certainly can. Like the riches to rags arc, the Icarus Pyramid might be used to paint different "what if" scenarios or picture of what things might be like for the audience if the Big Idea isn't implemented.

Examples of the Icarus Story Arc are *The Hunger Games* series by Suzanne Collins, which has a happy ending, and William Shakespeare's *Macbeth*, which has anything but a happy ending.

It shouldn't be surprising to hear that there is one story arc that has been named after an actual fairy tale. This is the **Cinderella arc**. This is an incredibly common arc that follows the hero or protagonist's rise to a new height, and be brought down very low, only to rise even higher than before. Emily Bronte's *Jane Eyre* and Disney's *Up* are both good examples of this arc, though they are probably of different literary merit. The Cinderella arc can be as effective in raising audience engagement as, say, the rags to riches story.

Type	Plot Diagram	Description	Example
01 Rags to Riches (Rise)		The hero typically starts with nothing and ends up living happily ever after.	• The Pursuit of Happyness • Les Miserables
02 Riches to Rags (Fall)		The hero starts with everything and then proceeds to lose it all.	• Rocky V • Schitt's Creek
03 Man in a Hole (Fall - Rise)		The most used out of all the story arcs. The hero experiences both good luck and bad luck.	• The Hobbit • Finding Nemo
04 Icarus / Freytag's Pyramid (Rise - Fall)		It's from the Greek tale of an imprisoned boy who builds wax wings to escape and eventually flies too close to the sun.	• Titanic • The Great Gatsby
05 Cinderella (Rise - Fall - Rise)		The hero proceeds to rise before falling and then rises again.	• Jane Eyre • Frozen
06 Oedipus (Fall - Rise - Fall)		Often used in tragedies and is one of the most difficult story arcs to pull off.	• The Godfather • Gone Girl

The final story arc at hand is one that has a bad ending. This is the **Oedipus arc.** As you may have guessed from its name, it's often used in tragedies like *Oedipus* and *Antigone*, and dramas. Telling a story with this kind of arc while keeping the story interesting is understandably difficult to pull off.

How Story Arcs Fit a Dramatic Structure

A dramatic structure is the thing that describes how a story moves along. Every one of the story arcs mentioned above makes use of one dramatic structure. The elements that make up a dramatic structure are exposition, inciting incident, rising action or progressive complications, dilemma, climax, and denouement. Before we explain what these elements are, here's how they would be plotted in, say, a rags to riches arc:

As for what exactly these elements are, the exposition is the scene setter. Its purpose is to introduce the world, including the setting and the characters of the story to the audience.

The inciting incident is the event or situation that kicks the plot into action. Meanwhile, the rising action is the upward movement of the story, meaning the developments that take place. The dilemma is the point in the story where the characters have to make a choice and when combined with the climax creates a moment of high tension and action. The climax is the tensest, make-it-or-break-it moment of the story. From there, things will either improve for the characters or they will deteriorate.

Finally, the denouement is the end of the story where everything is resolved and the plot wraps up.

These elements of the dramatic structure exist in every possible arc. In fact, they give each arc their own structure. Interestingly enough, story arcs can actually be divided into three-act structures. These three acts are the beginning, middle, and end of a story. It works for any story and arc, allows you the flexibility to use whatever arc you want in your story, and gives you a framework to use as you work with your audiences' expectations.

Usually, 25% of the story arc takes place in the first act, 50% takes place in the middle act and the last 25% takes place in the final act, though there are exceptions (Boyd, 2020). The most complicated arcs, for instance, sometimes have as many as nine acts in the form of three three-act structures. The longer a series or epic is, the more complicated patterns the arcs will combine in, creating 12, 18, or maybe even 27 acts.

Now, every story needs conflict. What kind of conflict does your story need, seeing as you're not exactly writing a fictional novel? The kind of conflict you need in your story is one that is positioned between your values and their counterpoint. But what values?

Well, a story arc rises and falls around six values (Coyne, 2015). These six values are:

- Physiological needs, like the need for food, water, and shelter.
- The need for safety, which can mean both personal safety and group security.
- The need for love/belonging, which is the value that's derived from friendships, families, relationships, and even communities.
- The need for esteem, which is the value of personal accomplishment and prestige as opposed to failure.
- The need for self-actualization, which is the ability to fulfill your true potential.
- The need for transcendence, which is the value found in becoming more than yourself.

Now, most novels and films are made by combining three plots, three different value scales like the ones listed above:

- main plot
- internal plot
- sub-plot

Each of these plots must have their own arc. That means that if you are writing an adventure story and if a coming of age story and love story both are integral to it, as in the Alchemist and A Tale of Two Cities, then you will have one arc per plot. Meaning, you will have three different arcs.

How to Adopt Story Arcs Into Your STC Horizontal Structure

Now that you understand the six main arcs and how they interact with the core values of stories, the question is how do you actually use this information to write great stories in STC?

Overall, there are six practices you can adopt to accomplish this:

- **Make sure your story moves.** The story you're telling—be it an example you're giving that can prove the point you're making during your presentation or an anecdote you're sharing in your slides to show how a particular problem can be solved—can take a positive or negative turn somewhere close to its beginning, ideally after the exposition has taken place and the scene has been set. What matters is that it takes some kind of turn and thus, moves along. A narrative that stays the same is not a story but simply an account of events.

- **Don't worry about matching your case study story to a particular arc in your first draft:** You may know what your case study is and how its arc will unfold when you sit down to write. In other words, you may know when to introduce conflict, which illustrates the problem your presentation aims to solve,, for instance, and the resolution you're offering your audience. You may know when to begin introducing your big idea too. Then again you may not. Don't worry too much about it. Just focus on telling your story. Remember, if you have a clear idea of your story, you don't need to worry too much about whether it matches the arcs above.

- **In your first draft, do worry about finding what your main message is:** While you don't need to worry about the exact shape the story you're telling will take when you start writing, you should try to discover what its main message is. To that end, you should ask yourself what idea your story revolves around? What's at its very center or core? If you can discover that, you will be much better equipped to make sure it moves the way it needs to.

- **Write toward the story's dilemma:** You don't need to know everything that's going to say in every single chart right at the set, down to the smallest detail. But you should still know what your central dilemma—the problem you're trying to solve or the message you're trying to give—will be. Your dilemma is the turning point of your story. It's the point that your presentation has to solve or the new idea it has to introduce to bring about the kind of change your audience wants. It's what will determine your protagonist's—your audience's—ultimate fate. This moment is usually at the very bottom of a dip in a story arc. Alternatively, it may be found at its zenith. Both these points are great for introducing your problem. It will be followed almost immediately by a climax, meaning the solution you're offering or the overall message you're trying to give. If you can find what your dilemma is, you will have found your story.

- **In your second draft, find each arc and enhance them:** You don't need to know the shape of your main story arc or the sub-arcs in your first draft. Once you move onto your second draft, on the other hand, you do need to find your arc. Ask yourself what its shape is. How does it rise? How does it fall? Does it fall as much as it should? Could it rise more? Is there enough movement to it?

Using Case Studies and Stories With Emotional Triggers

In Hollywood and in marketing, the most powerful stories are ones that draw on real-life personal experiences. Drawing from your experiences, though, can be rather difficult to do in a corporate organization. So what should you do instead? You can use case studies. Granted, case studies are not powerful emotional triggers as personal experiences are, but they can be made to be so. This effect can especially reach its maximum when you present in person.

Having said all this, you might still be wondering how story arcs apply to STC. We're not writing fiction, after all. Well, we may not be writing fiction, but we will still be using various case studies in our presentations. We will have to as they are important, illustrative proofs of the points that we are trying to make. Case studies are significant tools that are often used by strategy consultants to draw on the best practices and lessons learned. Unfortunately, a lot of people tend to write their case studies in a really, very dull way, if we're being honest. That's where story arcs come in. Story arcs can be used when sharing and describing case studies to add some much-needed color and vividness to them. This would make them far more interesting and engaging, which would in turn draw your audience further into your presentation. A dull description of a case study, on the other hand, would not.

Putting people's stories in charts without appearing unprofessional is both very difficult and rather unconventional. To stop that from being the case, you should use voiceover over charts and inject other people's and groups' relevant stories and experiences there. That doesn't mean you should only use case studies when you're speaking to your audience in person. But it does mean that speaking to your audience directly can help you personalize case studies more as you present. For example, if you are using a chart like the one below to illustrate an experience, you can use voiceover to explain how you met the owners or managers of a case, and what happened to them.

We were once engaged by the owners and the board of a private hospital situated in one of the most expensive cities in the country, offering the most expensive real estate in the world. The hospital had 85% occupancy but was only breaking even then. The figures at hand showed that at 85%, it should've made a handsome profit. Needless to say, we got hired to look into what was happening internally that was keeping the hospital from making that profit. At first, when we were interviewing hospital staff, we couldn't really identify an issue. Later, it turned out that the CEO of the hospital had been terrorizing the staff so that they wouldn't say anything. The staff had been effectively conditioned to tell us that everything was fine. What's more, the CEO had carefully handpicked the people we could see in the hospital. After we finished our engagement, the CEO had a heart attack. This happened after we finalized our project and submitted our findings to the board of directors. The board of directors then made the decision to limit the CEO's authority and stipulated that he now had to get additional approvals from the board for various things that used to be under his sole discretion. The CEO felt betrayed by the board and the staff as a result of this decision. Hence the heart attack. To this day, I feel responsible for that and can't get over the fact that our engagement might have caused it. This, right here, is the kind of real-life emotional story that would be voiced over during an in-person presentation, and not be put into the copy of a slide.

The Hero's Journey

As discussed earlier, stories are powerful techniques that can be adopted to influence people by relating to them. Well-crafted and narrated stories have the powerful ability to engage audiences and channel their attention to your presentation. The story is made up of a series of sentences, known as action titles, captions, headers, lead-ins, story arcs, and more. It also has a component to it called the hero's journey, which is made up of specific milestones, while still being entirely unique.

A single story has the power to captivate a whole audience, but only if it's done correctly. Here's where the "hero's journey" comes to play. This is the common template of storytelling used in films, books, and marketing, to name but a few examples. This template has been the go-to for almost every storyteller ever since the legendary Joseph Campbell introduced it. In one of the most influential books of the 20th century, *The Hero with a Thousand Faces*, he introduced his readers to the hero's journey. The ideas presented by Campbell were not entirely original though. They were already in existence and being used by pretty much everyone and anyone telling stories, whether they realized it or not. What Campbell did, though, was to recognize the pattern, expose it, articulate it, name it, and publicize it.

Campbell was heavily influenced by Swiss psychologist Carl Jung's archetypes. These archetypes had the same repeating characters appear in the dreams of all people. They came from a deeper source in the collective unconscious of the human race. Stories are the same. The same repeating story and characters follow the same pattern of myths, whether deliberately or unconsciously. That is why the hero has a thousand faces.

The hero's journey consists of three main parts, which can be utilized to improve, analyze, and create narratives in countless ways:

- **The separation:** The hero sets off on whatever journey they have been put on, thus separating from all that they know—including the known, familiar world and the people they love, like their family, in search of adventure, even if they do so reluctantly at the time. Within the context of STC, this would be the reason why your audience needs to separate themselves from the existing methodologies, solutions, or strategies within their market and try something wholly different.

- **The initiation:** The voyage that the hero or protagonist ends up taking and the series of fortunate and the series of fortunate and unfortunate events that take place during, all ultimately leading them to their destination or goal. Within the context of STC, this would be the journey your audience would take to implement your Big Idea and how your presentation would unfold to convince them that they should implement it.

- **The return:** The hero or protagonist's return home or to the known world in some form or fashion, after they have completed their voyage and attained or achieved what they were after. Within the context of STC, this would be what would happen after the audience implemented whatever Big Idea, ideas, or solution you were offering them.

Once you really get the hang of using the hero's journey, you'll realize how important it truly is. Once you start incorporating this horizontal logic hack into your presentations, you'll see what an incredible and how big of an impact it will leave on your audience.

To understand the Hero's Journey concept a bit better, here's how it might look in STC:

Stage	Description	Example
The Ordinary World	This is the hero's initial reality, which lacks something. This stage allows the audience to get to know the hero and empathize with him before going on his journey.	The audience's current reality, which either lacks something or is faced with a problem, is presented.
The Call to Adventure	Every story has a problem or a central dramatic question that disrupts the ordinary world. Here a challenge, problem, or adventure is thrown at the hero. The hero's goal is established at this stage.	A distress call or reason to enact some kind of change to alter the world in which the audience lives in is given.
The Refusal of the Call	The (often hesitant) hero refuses to call to adventure and prefers to stay in his safe, ordinary world. He considers the risks. This is a crucial stage that discusses the possible failure of the task. Without it, the audience will not be compelled to keep up with the hero's journey.	A possible obstacle that might make the audience resistant or hesitant to enact change is explained.
Meeting with the Mentor	The hero meets a wise figure (could also be a physical object or a symbolic figure too) who helps him prepare for the adventure. This figure offers advice, assistance, and insight into the new world the hero's about to embark on.	The presenter, in the role of the "mentor" figure, addresses the obstacle, explains why change is necessary, and debunks the beliefs that may have led to this hesitancy, giving examples to back up their words where necessary.

Stage	Description	Example
Crossing the Threshold	The hero has committed to his mission and entered the new world, and at this point, there's no turning back. A threshold guardian often meets him.	The initial steps the audience might take to enact change or an idea are delved into.
Tests, Allies, and Enemies	The hero learns the new laws of his new world by meeting new people and gathering further information. He undergoes tests, encounters allies, and confronts enemies. This stage is especially important because it is when the hero's true personal characteristics shine through.	The potential obstacles, resistant beliefs, and difficulties to realizing the Big Idea or the 5 Ideas are outlined and made clear.
Approach to the Innermost Cave	The hero, with his allies, has arrived at the edge of the most dangerous location where the "object of the quest" is hidden.	The main message and goal of the presentation is given and the Big Idea is explained.
The Ordeal	The hero is in danger, often in a physical or psychological life-or-death situation. At this point, the hero is on the brink of failure.	The biggest obstacle to the implementation of the Big Idea or the main message is explored.
Reward or Seizing the Sword	The hero survives death. He receives his reward, which can be treasure, weapon, knowledge, token, reconciliation, etc.	The rewards of enacting the Big Idea or main message are laid out.
The Road Back	The hero now has to cope with the consequences of his actions. He must now choose whether or not to return to the ordinary world.	The new reality that the audience will face as a result of the implemented main message or Big Idea is discussed.

Stage	Description	Example
Resurrection	The hero must pass one more tests, the most dangerous one yet. It is his final ordeal before he's purified and reborn or before he undergoes a transformation.	The challenges that the audience will have to face when adapting to the changes that are taking place as a result of having implemented the Big Idea are explored.
Return with the Elixir	The victorious hero returns to the ordinary world with the elixir. Treasure, love, freedom, wisdom, and knowledge are all common elixirs. All storylines are resolved, the ordinary world is restored, and the hero can now begin a new life, forever changed by the journey.	The ultimate goal and result that the audience wants to achieve is described, as is how the presented ideas and messages will help achieve them.

Copy Hacks and Subliminal Strategies to Keep Emotions on a Trigger

The art of the copy is a vast subject area that has been claimed by many a guru, ranging from classic legends like David Ogilvy and Eugene Schwartz to countless modern-day copywriters. The topic has been mostly exploited in the context of direct response marketing. You won't find much material on how you can exploit the art of copywriting in storytelling beyond advertising, sales, and marketing. Throughout this book, however, you'll find bits and pieces of how I adapt this knowledge to craft better presentations and storytelling with charts. The intent of this section here is to give you some tips and hacks that I have not covered in detail so far and which you can adopt to augment your storytelling by a notch. As an example, let's say that I am using the hospital case in the above example as a case study in a presentation. In this scenario, the heart attack bit of the story would not be written down on a slide as I presented it. Instead, it would be something I shared during a presentation in a voice-over format, as though I were presenting it to my audience, in person.

On an individual level, copy hacks might not make too big an impact. But if you mix and match them by combining several within a story, you'll manage to keep your audience engaged. You'll also be able to make the experience of going through the content memorable and pleasant.

The Bridge From the Story to the Pitch Paint a Picture Using Contrast

Ultimately, whatever your presentation or report is about, there's always something you want. That something is your goal, which you identified at the very start of the STC process, and it usually rises to the surface in your attempts to convince your audience to take action in some way. This thing you're asking for might be a sale, a recommendation, a funding request, a change of course, new findings, a strategy, or a solution to a problem. Whatever it is, the one thing that won't change is that you'll need to convince your audience to accept it.

Sigmund Freud is thought to have said, "We are so constituted that we can gain intense pleasure only from the contrast, and only very little from the condition itself." The biggest mistake people make when trying to convince others of something is to try and show them the features and not the benefits of what they're offering. This is a mistake because it is not nearly as effective as painting a picture of the benefit in emotional triggers. When you paint a picture, you make the state of something immediately visible. You give your audience the ability to use their senses and so feel, hear, taste, experience, and see what you're talking about. Experiencing something in this way obviously ends up becoming far more convincing than just listening to its benefits.

Start with your audience's current reality and paint the picture as it currently is. Let's call this "Point A." Then contrast that with the desire that the audience really has, meaning what they really want. That's "Point B". Our messages and other content draw attention to the relationship between what they have vs. what they want. You want to draw a line between those two points and that line is the tension. It's the feeling and thought, "Just for a moment I want you to imagine what it would feel like."

Who?	Not what you think	Primary Goal	Secondary Goal
Persona	What they need	What they really want	What they ultimately really want
Young Professional	To buy a luxury sports car	To turn heads, attract the opposite or same sex	Impress others, secure a date
Reader of This Book	To learn to write stories with charts really fast	To captivate the audience and persuade them to act	Recognition, status, wealth, relationship
Sales Professional	Sell a product or service	To make the numbers, get promoted, achieve quota and get paid a high bonus	Freedom, wealth
Entrepreneur	Build a successful company	Grow or sell a business	Secure wealth and an early retirement
Middle–Aged Person	Luxury convertible and to ditch old family car	Be reborn, feel young again	To buy a new identity
Overweight Individual	To lose weight	To fit back into their old clothes	To reclaim the energy of their youth

In the earlier example of Luke Skywalker was a farmer who became a Jedi master. Before he achieved this, though, he had to first rescue Princess Leia, join the Rebel Alliance, and blow up the Death Star. That's the kind of journey that you want to try to take your audience through, except with fewer Death Stars. The remarkable strategy that's used in Star Wars is the recursivity that's seen in the journey, that is to say the journey within the journey. This is an advanced concept in scriptwriting where the idea is to use contrast within a contrast within a contrast.

What all this means is that you should allocate some time during your planning process and the process of structuring your story to identify what your contrasts are. You should then include them in the structuring of your messages. Your individual ideas can thus be augmented substantially to trigger emotions and engagement through these subliminal messages, which are given to your audience's subconscious, influencing their emotions, thoughts, and therefore decision-making process.

Show Empathy

It's not your fault. As a young consultant, I was eager to develop a presentation that showed no regard for my clients' feelings. I thought that was what I was supposed to do. But the thing is, the people who you investigate for your presentation are the very people who will have to make the change that you're recommending. If you make a recommendation to them that doesn't take their feelings into account, then those people will be resistant to whatever you're suggesting, even if that thing would be immensely useful to them. If, on the other hand, you not only understood their feelings, that is to say, empathized with them, but made them part of the presentation? Then you would use your audience's feelings as a way to make them connect more to your suggestions and let go of any resistance or objections they might have by making them feel seen and understood. Put simply, if you don't show empathy in your presentation, your recommendation will end up failing.

If you don't show empathy, your recommendation will end up failing.

Mix Between System 1, Keep From Always Giving the Answer in Metaphors to Engage System 2 Less

This might sound like it's counterintuitive. It might also sound like it's contradicting my previous recommendation about the importance of not falling "for the knowledge trap." However, that's not actually the case here. For simplicity's sake, say you want your audience to imagine that you were trying to say the "number 4," without writing down the number "4." One way to do this would be to write "1+3" instead wouldn't it? This way, you would force your audience to think just a little bit and engage them mentally. This will keep them alert and attentive. You shouldn't get carried away with this trick, though, and expect them to guess what "28x74" equals. Doing that would strain their thinking and you want to go for ease, not strain, as you'll remember from earlier conversations.

Happy Mood and Humor

This is a rather difficult hack as some people may consider humor to be unprofessional when it's used in a professional presentation. However, depending on what setting you're in, you can infuse your presentation with humor, even if it appears like this was done unintentionally. I always find one or two charts at the beginning of the presentation that could get the audience in a good mood before diving into the meat of the content. Putting the audience in a good mood like this relaxes them and makes them far more open to hearing the ideas I have to share with them. In other words, it whittles down resistance to a degree.

Tackle New Information With "Cognitive Ease" and Through Repetition

If you're exposed to something over and over, you're likely to remember or like it more. New information, on the other hand, will typically be perceived as a threat. The more that information is repeated, though, the less "new" it comes. The less new it comes, the less of a threat it constitutes. As such, repeating the information you share in presentations several times is very important. Doing so will both ensure that your audience will remember it more and be less put off by it. Therefore they'll be less resistant to it and the suggestions you'll make on account of that new info.

Cognitive Ease

Decorrelating efforts is a sound way of solidifying your presentation. It's also a great way of increasing your presentation's cognitive ease. To understand what cognitive ease is, we can look at an experiment scientists once conducted, where participants were briefly shown pictures of various objects. Sometimes they showed the outlines of the objects in the picture before showing the pictures themselves. The outlines were only shown in flashes though, so the participants were only able to notice their basic contours. While this was going on, scientists measured the electrical impulses in their facial muscles. In doing so, they discovered that participants displayed faint smiles when the outlines flashed by, because this made the pictures easier to see. System 1 effectively kicked in at these moments, because cognitive ease was taking place and so generated good feelings (Winkielman & Cacioppo, 2001).

Cognitive ease may take many forms. How easy a company's name is to pronounce, for example, can trigger cognitive ease or strain. Given that, if a company with an unpronounceable name like Zgjharl were to offer stocks, they likely wouldn't do very well in the long run. Meanwhile, a stock with pronounceable names like MANEE for instance would outperform tongue twisters such as Zgjharl.

Cognitive ease is a must for presentations, as you'll remember. This is because it makes it easy for your audience to keep paying attention to your presentation. It also makes it easier for them to become invested in it and to fully absorb the concepts and ideas that you introduce. So what does all this mean? Essentially, it means that you need to be careful what kind of words and language you use in your presentation. Using words, metaphors, and sentences that are too complicated to be understood is a surefire way of losing audience engagement and ensuring your story and objective fail.

Metaphors

Metaphors are incredibly effective storytelling tools that can accomplish two major things simultaneously. They can connect the unknown to the known and they can connect the known to the unknown. What does that mean? To understand that, let's look at what a metaphor is. A metaphor is an analogy that is able to synthesize two different concepts. They can do this by taking a very complicated and convoluted idea or theory, simplifying it, and thus turning it into something immediately graspable. This is what's meant by connecting the unknown to the known. This ability that metaphors possess helps you to simplify your big idea and make it familiar to your audience. As such, it's very useful when you're trying to convey your idea, hypothesis, strategies and more. At the same time, metaphors can do things like hide or conceal an idea inside something that looks to be common. In doing so, they can generate a sense of mystery and thus curiosity, which will serve to engage and intrigue your audience.

There is such a thing as framing effects. Framing effects are different ways of presenting the same information to an audience to evoke different emotions in them. Let's take the statement "the odds of survival one month after surgery are 90%" as an example. Typically, this will be construed as a reassuring statement, since it means that the odds of mortality are low. However, put a different way, it could be used to stress that there is a risk of death post-surgery. Stressing that 10% in this way could evoke fear and worry, as opposed to relief and reassurance.

What this means in the context of STC is that you can convey data in a myriad of ways. Once you've obtained the data you need, think carefully about how you can present and discuss it. What feelings do you want to evoke? How can you format and phrase this data in a way that you can actually evoke those feelings? What metaphors can you use to make those feelings immediately communicable?

Priming

The psychologic John Bargh once asked his students to put together two sentences made up of four-letter words using a set of five words. One group of students were given a set of words that pertained to the elderly, though neither the word "elderly" nor "old" were included in this set. Once they were done, they were sent out of the room to take a walk and the second group came in. Unbeknownst to the first group, the point of the experiment was the talk that the groups took following the word experiment. This is because scientists wanted to see whether the kinds of words the groups dealt with would affect their behavior in any way.

To their surprise, they found that it did. The scientists observed that the time it took the first group to get from one end of the corridor to the other was much slower than the time it took the second group, who dealt with entirely different words. What Bargh and his team discovered is that the words (and things) that we are exposed to prime our behavior in unique ways. When we sort through a bunch of words that have to do with the elderly, our behavior and actions slow down. Similarly, when we deal with words associated with youth and energy, on the other hand, they speed up. Following his experiment, Bargh dubbed This phenomenon the Florida Effect and it is a perfect example of the psychological condition known as "priming" (Schimmack, 2017).

The Florida Effect typically unfolds in two stages. In the first stage, the set of words people are given primes their thoughts. In the case of this group, their thoughts were primed for old age. In the second, the thoughts people have prime their behavior. Again, in this example, the old-age thoughts primed the group's behavior, thus causing them to slow down the way elderly people would. When the students in the experiment were questioned about this, they stated that they hadn't realized there had been any change in their behavior. That they didn't notice though doesn't mean such a change didn't take place.

As you might have surmised from all this, priming is a powerful hack you can use in STC. By choosing the right set of words and using them in your presentation often, you can prime your audience's thoughts. To do this, think of what action you want your audience to ultimately take. Now, take out a pen and paper and work on a word tree. What words can be associated with that behavior? Once you have your list, choose the best ones and take care to use them throughout your presentation and your charts.

Don't Have Too Many Choices

Presenting your audience with too many choices to choose from is something you absolutely want to avoid doing in STC. This is because too many choices create a kind of paradox. Dr. Barry Schwartz demonstrates as much in his book, The Paradox of Choice. Having too many choices isn't actually something that makes us any happier, as Schwartz demonstrates. In fact, our brains have a subconscious preference for fewer choices. This is despite the fact that we sometimes complain that our choices are limited (Schwartz, 2016).

Strategy consultants like me often get into the habit of recommending a "best option" so to speak, if we have many different options at hand. To choose the best option, you have to use simple, defined guiding principles that are either agreed upon or are indisputable to your audience. Then, you evaluate these options according to these criteria. You can assign each option you have a numerical value based on this assessment and choose the option with the highest grade. Alternatively, you can also filter out some of your options based on what your "must" criteria are, thereby reducing the number of options that are available to you.

If you have multiple strategies and solutions to present to your audience, take a moment to reconsider them carefully in this way. If you give your audience too many such choices, they will become paralyzed and be unable to make any kind of decision. If, on the other hand, you were to narrow down your choices to the best handful of options, then you would make the process of selection much easier for your audience. They would therefore become much more likely to choose at least one of the options you've presented them with.

Polarizing Messages

Adding polarizing messages to your story not only triggers emotions, but also increases engagement. As discussed earlier, in various experiments our brains are programmed to notice and pick up on negative emotions before positive ones. As such if you want to guide your audience toward the behaviors you want them to adopt, you need to first activate their negative emotions. These emotions, like anger or fear, for example, will make them want to avoid the situation that is associated with them. This will likely be the situation that you've been tasked with changing in the first place. As an example, you might not be all that surprised that companies who try to sell certain products or services to their clients often trigger negative surprises in them first. This way, they trigger a need to avoid the situation that evokes that feeling.

Of course, things just don't end at evoking a negative emotion. Once you have done that, you need to activate an approach associated with a positive emotion by presenting your solution to your audience's pain. This, of course, will liberate your audience from the tension you created by re-enacting their fears. Creating these tensions will make the audience experience a momentary emotional lift that will create trust, safety, joy, love, and excitement between you and them. This will, in turn, increase their likelihood of adopting your solution in the end.

The basic idea to remember here is that the three dimensions that play a part in creating captivating content include emotion, logic, and engagement. Your STC strategy and structure should, as much as possible, ensure all three dimensions are continuously in check.

Some emotions are of course more complicated than others. This is because emotions like happiness and fear are primary emotions. These emotions combine in different ways to create other, more complicated ones. If you're trying to evoke a complicated emotion in your audience, you need to understand what that emotion is a combo of. In doing so, you can figure out how you can evoke them. To accomplish this, you can make use of Plutchik's Wheel of Emotions. Some examples of how emotions may combine to create new ones might be (Williams, 2013):

Anger coupled with Anticipation equals	Aggressiveness
Sadness mixed with Disgust results in	Remorse
Anticipation combined Trust creates	Hope
Joy when added to fear Fear leads to	Guilt
Trust on top of Surprise generates	Curiosity
Fear mixed in with Sadness	Despair
Surprise and Disgust manifesting together leads to	Disbelief, Shock
Joy appearing alongside Surprise yields	Delight
Trust intermingling with Sadness births	Sentimentality
Fear combined Disgust fashions	Shame
Surprise plus Anger equals	Outrage

An ROT to remember here is that getting your audience in a good mood is so important. If you invoke a negative emotion in them, you need to make sure you offset that with a mix of positive ones while you maintain anticipation.

Always try and keep your audience in a good mood.

Recap

- You need to use a uniform structure all throughout your STC, no matter what your purpose, goal, or strategic objectives are.

- First impressions matter and impact the rest of your presentation and how your audience will respond to it.

- 80% of the content you will present in your study will be based on the 3DF. More or less 20% of it, meanwhile, will be dedicated to what actions you want your audience to take or what you expect from your audience, regardless of STC.

- The big idea is the one common threat that will be running through all of the individual messages you'll be giving throughout your story.

- Test your big idea by asking yourself if it's specific, contrarian, easy to articulate, and desirable. If not, work on it more.

- A big idea that is part of such a story is both emotionally compelling and makes a primary promise.

- Metaphors can connect the unknown to the known and they can connect the known to the unknown.

- To develop a big idea you need to start brainstorming and generate as many ideas as you possibly can.

- Your ability to generate a new idea from all of these different sources depends on two things: your creativity and your capacity to combine old, familiar elements in ways that allow you to see new relationships.

- Note the key proof points of all the ideas you come up with, as in literally writing them down. This will help you later. Make sure that those proof points are both emotionally and intellectually appealing.

- Remember that you are not writing a copy. This is simply developing the big idea, so you don't have to worry about being too verbose or anything like that (yet)

- Give yourself ample time to actually think on, research, and develop your big idea.

- Don't start expanding on your big idea until you feel the need to do so and you feel ready to do so. If you feel that you don't yet have enough information to be able to follow the concept through, then you likely don't.

- Do a test elevator pitch of your idea. This pitch should summarize your big idea in a concise—no more than two sentences long—and clear statement and express it powerfully but simply.

- Ask yourself what your audience believes and identify your own beliefs.

- The intro expands on your big idea and typically takes up the first two to five minutes of your story, depending on how long and complicated your story is. Those two to five minutes translate to your initial two to five slides or charts, depending on how complicated your intro and story are.

- Your right intro and title basically account for about 4% of your story. Yet they will account for 64% of its success.
- The executive summary refers to your next 5–30 charts or messages, following your intro.
- Having a good story to tell is important but what makes a story great is the narrative.
- The first thing I do when creating the intro is to open the loop with a big idea. You then close the loop at the very end of the presentation.
- Don't ever assume your audience knows everything that you know.
- To tell a good story, you need to craft a solid story arc that describes the shape of the change you aim to see and its value throughout the entirety of that story.
- A dramatic structure is the thing that describes how a story moves along.
- The hero's journey is a 12-step process that you can use to tell your own story.
- You should case studies and stories with emotional triggers for audience engagement.
- You need to empathize with your audience if you want to keep their attention.
- Use humor to put your audience in a good mood when it's appropriate.
- Use the halo effect to your benefit as you structure the flow of your story.
- Start with a negative feeling and then follow it up with a positive one, thereby making use of the negativity bias.
- Prime your audience's thoughts and behavior by using the right words, associated with the action you want them to take, throughout the presentation.
- Don't offer your audience too many choices, lest they experience choice paralysis.
- Use polarizing messages to maximize the emotional effect you have on your audience.

Chapter 6: Pulling It All Together

A framework is a roadmap, not a restriction. –Jeff Bezos

Now that you've reached this part of the book, I hope you found this tutorial helpful. I must confess that conclusions are not my strongest suit. However, in this particular moment, if you have reached this point after completing the book—meaning if you didn't open this chapter before completing all previous chapters—then you've likely arrived at the most important part of *Storytelling With Charts*. This is because this chapter puts together everything you've learned up till now in a single unified system, as illustrated in the progress flow map below. If you have not been able to piece the individual frameworks together in your mind yet, this chapter will help you accomplish that.

Putting It All Together

All in all, this STC tutorial can be a summary of the STC system or framework whose process and flow are mapped as shown below. The system boils down to 5 phases consisting of 17 steps through an overall iterative and dynamic process:

STC Entire Process Flow Map

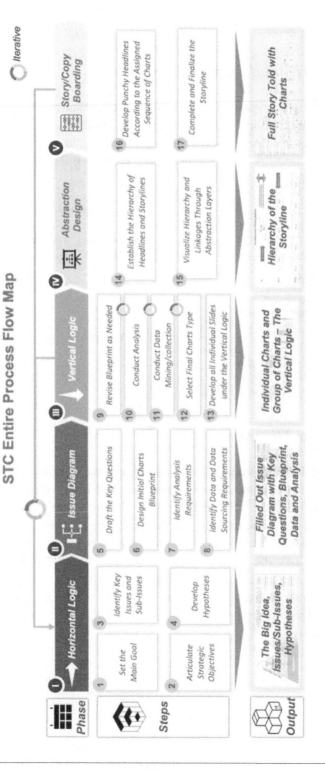

○ Iterative

Phase

I — Horizontal Logic

II ⊩ Issue Diagram

III → Vertical Logic

IV Abstraction Design

V Story/Copy Boarding

Steps

1 Set the Main Goal
2 Articulate Strategic Objectives
3 Identify Key Issues and Sub-Issues
4 Develop Hypotheses

5 Draft the Key Questions
6 Design Initial Charts Blueprint
7 Identify Analysis Requirements
8 Identify Data and Data Sourcing Requirements

9 Revise Blueprint as Needed
10 Conduct Analysis
11 Conduct Data Mining/collection
12 Select Final Charts Type
13 Develop all Individual Slides under the Vertical Logic

14 Establish the Hierarchy of Headlines and Storylines
15 Visualize Hierarchy and Linkages Through Abstraction Layers

16 Develop Punchy Headlines According to the Assigned Sequence of Charts
17 Complete and Finalize the Storyline

Output

The Big Idea, Issues/Sub-Issues, Hypotheses

Filled Out Issue Diagram with Key Questions, Blueprint, Data and Analysis

Individual Charts and Group of Charts – The Vertical Logic

Hierarchy of the Storyline

Full Story Told with Charts

231

The Horizontal Logic Development

In Phase I, the horizontal logic is developed by starting out with the goal and the preliminary strategic objectives. Your issues, sub-issues, and hypotheses are drawn out of these. The main idea of this phase is to develop a long list of hypotheses that cover all possible root causes and of the issues and sub-issues.

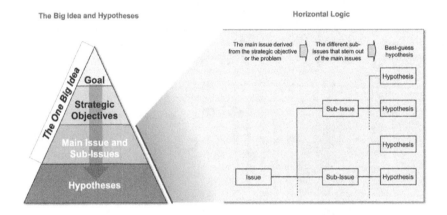

The Issue Diagram

In Phase II, you expand the "Issue Diagram," fill out and identify key questions, design the charts, blueprint, and identify data and analysis requirements. The idea here is not to do the work, but to plan it out. Filling out the issue diagram implies determining, for example, the kind of analysis you need to conduct and the kind of data you will need. This, however, isn't the time you do the actual data and analysis. That will come in the next step as you go through the vertical slides development. Doing so not only helps you plan your work, but also, if you have a team or other team members working, allocate each of these tasks to the team members.

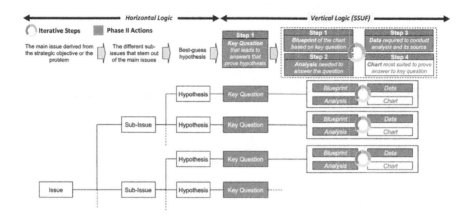

The Vertical Logic

In Phase III, all charts need to support your hypotheses and claims in the form of vertical logic slides. These should follow the instructions given in the Phase II issue diagram. This stage is as simple as executing or implementing the issue diagram in order to design the slides required for vertical logic, answering the Key Question, and proving the hypotheses under the issue.

As discussed in the earlier chapter, it's important to note that vertical logic is an iterative phase and includes iterative steps. You need to run this iteration and confirm that everything continues to hold logically as you develop your verticals. You also need to make sure they align with the horizontal logic and link back to the main goal and strategic objectives that you had already identified.

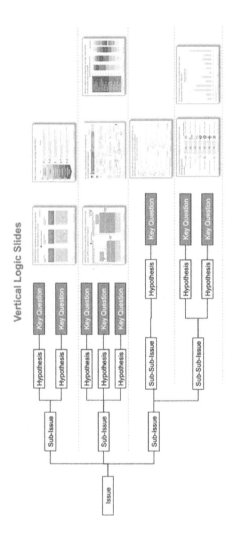

The Abstract Design

In Phase IV, you apply abstract thinking to finalize the hierarchy of your storyline. At this stage, the hierarchy of messages includes stories within stories, and nonlinear dependencies as well as hypotheses and issues whose linkages may not be as apparent. Establishing and visualizing a clear hierarchy of stories and issues is essential to structuring the flow of your entire story. As such, you need to do this before proceeding to the final phase of copy boarding and storyboarding.

Copy/Storyboarding

Phase V is the last and most important phase in the whole process. It's where you take the plain hypotheses, statements, and claims and convert them into punchy headlines according to the flow and the assigned sequence of charts you had developed in the previous phase. It's important that this final phase is iterated with the very first phase in order to ensure that every headline message is run through the "So what factor" and to ensure that they link directly or indirectly back to the goal and strategic objectives.

When you gain more experience with the STC method, you'll intuitively be able to start your horizontal logic by storyboarding your story. But I don't recommend you start learning the STC method like this. You shouldn't forget, meanwhile, that you can always use mind maps to visualize and run through your story to make sure it flows naturally and logically.

The "So What?" Factor

The "So What?" factor is an important aspect of STC that deserves to be recapped. The factor centers on the question "So What?"

Answering this question is the challenge you have to pose yourself and others at the end of every slide. So, you should read the header out loud and ask yourself, so what? Doing this basically gets you to ask another, essential question to yourself about your work:

Does this slide strengthen my objective?

If the slide doesn't bring anything to the table, then you need to either eliminate or turn it into a backup slide.

Making STC Stick

Before signing off, I will leave you with this: I was born in Brazil, and only spoke Portuguese until the age of five, after which, my parents decided to move to Lebanon. Very few people have vivid memories of that age, but I do. I recall that period so well because I had a hard time making and retaining friends, since I could hardly communicate with anyone. My biggest problem was school, where everything was taught in either French or Arabic.

At that age, though, the human brains develop incredibly quickly, and you tend to learn fast. So a few months later, I started to gain some fluency in both languages until they both came second nature to me. Unfortunately, I had to leave the country at the age of 17 and head to Germany, where the languages I spoke didn't really serve me in any way. So, here I was again, learning a new language. Luckily, I found that I had a talent for picking up languages very quickly, and within one year, I was fluent in German. You could say that I was a natural. My German got so good, you couldn't even tell I wasn't a native speaker.

Five years later, I moved to the United States, where I had to pick another new language one more time. At the age of 24, I learned English quickly. I was convinced that I had a talent for languages now. Fast forward 10 years, when I took my trip back to Lebanon. I arrived at the airport, and found out that I could not string together a full sentence in Arabic anymore. I struggled to put together the words! So what had happened to a language that was supposed to be my native tongue? I had forgotten how to speak it.

The moral of the story is that if you are using this book and will never practice what you've learned, you're most likely not going to retain anything. So, you'd better start putting what you learned in practice immediately if you want to make them stick.

Consider Repeating This Book and/or Purchasing the Toolkit

Personally, I suggest you put what you've learned into practice immediately. As such, you may want to consider re-reading this book at least once more. Your first read should've taken you around 2-3 hours max to complete.

Although tutorials are not the most suited topics to put in STC, I did make considerable effort to reduce the amount of reading required and include as many charts as possible. My intent was to switch your consumption to a visual mode rather than bore you through reading all the time. I figured that this way you could go through the content quickly, absorb it fast and retain it all at the end. Consider the additional time spent in repeating it a small investment in getting the hang of everything.

In addition to this, you can consider spending a few extra bucks to purchase the full toolkit that supplements this tutorial. This toolkit includes a video tutorial which changes your consumption of the framework to the audio-visual mode and may help you retain information even better. There is additional supplemental content there that's highly valuable, including a number of handy tools to immediately take your proficiency in STC to the next level.

Among others, the toolkit includes free form templates, a video tutorial, cheat sheets, presentations, templates, quantitative chart templates, and more. These are designed to let you hit the ground running. Upon completing the video tutorials, you'll be able to take your level to proficiency within just a few hours.

You can access the toolkit by going to:

www.storytellingwithcharts.com/toolkit

Recap
- The STC system or framework is made up of 5 phases consisting of 17 steps through an overall iterative and dynamic process.
- Phase I, the horizontal logic is developed by starting out with the goal and the preliminary strategic objectives. Your issues, sub-issues, and hypotheses are drawn out of these.
- In Phase II, you expand the "Issue Diagram," fill out and identify key questions, design the charts blueprint, and identify data and analysis requirements.
- In Phase III, all charts need to support your hypotheses and claims in the form of vertical logic slides.
- In Phase IV, you apply abstract thinking to finalize the hierarchy of your storyline. At this stage, the hierarchy of messages includes stories within stories, and nonlinear dependencies as well as hypotheses and issues whose linkages may not be as apparent.
- Phase V is the last and most important phase where you take the plain hypotheses, statements, and claims and convert them into punchy headlines according to the flow and the assigned sequence of charts you had developed in the previous phase.

References

- Anderson, J. A. E., Hawrylewicz, K., & Grundy, J. G. (2020). Does bilingualism protect against dementia? A meta-analysis. Psychonomic Bulletin & Review. doi.org/10.3758/s13423-020-01736-5

- Bar-Yam, Y. (2011). Concepts: power law. New England Complex Systems Institute. https://necsi.edu/power-law

- Baumeister, R. F., Bratslavsky, E., Finkenauer, C., & Vohs, K. D. (2001). Bad is Stronger than Good. Review of General Psychology, 5(4), 323–370. doi.org/10.1037/1089-2680.5.4.323

- Begg, I., Armour, V., & Kerr, T. (1985). On believing what we remember. Canadian Journal of Behavioural Science / Revue Canadienne Des Sciences Du Comportement, 17(3), 199–214. doi.org/10.1037/h0080140

- Benoît Mandelbrot. (2006). The fractal geometry of nature. W.H. Freeman And Company.

- Boudry, M., & Braeckman, J. (2012). How convenient! The epistemic rationale of self-validating belief systems. Philosophical Psychology, 25(3), 341–364. doi.org/10.1080/09515089.2011.579420

- Boyd, R. L., Blackburn, K. G., & Pennebaker, J. W. (2020). The narrative arc: Revealing core narrative structures through text analysis. Science Advances, 6(32), eaba2196. doi.org/10.1126/sciadv.aba2196

- Buck, R., & Oatley, K. (2007). Robert Plutchik (1927-2006). APA PsycNet.

- Burch, R. (2014). Charles Sanders Peirce (Stanford Encyclopedia of Philosophy). Stanford.edu. https://plato.stanford.edu/entries/peirce/

- Campbell, W. J. (2020, June 12). "Too tight": The botched glove demonstration at O.J. "Trial of the Century" in 1995. https://1995blog.com/2020/06/12/recalling-botched-glove-demonstration-at-1995-o-j-simpson-trial-of-the-century

- Chamberlain, R. (2019, September 23). How to transform dualistic thinking. Association of Corporate Counsel (ACC). https://www.acc.com/resource-library/how-transform-dualistic-thinking

- Clinton Eye Associates. (n.d.). Color blindness. Clinton Eye Associates. https://www.clintoneye.com/color-blindness.html

- Cothran, H. M., & Wysocki, A. F. (2019). Developing SMART Goals for Your Organization. EDIS, 2005(14). https://doi.org/10.32473/edis-fe577-2005

- Cowan, N. (2010). The Magical Mystery Four: How Is Working Memory Capacity Limited, and Why? Current Directions in Psychological Science, 19(1), 51–57. doi.org/10.1177/0963721409359277
- Coyne, S. (2015). The story grid : what good editors know. Black Irish Entertainment.
- Fincher, D. (Director). (2008). The Curious Case of Benjamin Button. Paramount Pictures.
- Goldman, A. (1964). Lindy's Law. The New Republic. https://www.gwern.net/docs/statistics/probability/1964-goldman.pdf
- Greenwood, J. (1998). The role of reflection in single and double loop learning. Journal of Advanced Nursing, 27(5), 1048–1053. doi.org/10.1046/j.1365-2648.1998.t01-1-00579.x
- Grigorieva, X. (2015). Pareto optimality in static competitive model of decision-making. Applied Mathematical Sciences, 9, 6217–6223. doi.org/10.12988/ams.2015.56463
- Harari, Y. N., Purcell, J., & Watzman, H. (2018). Sapiens : a brief history of humankind. Harper Perennial.
- Ho, L. (2020, September 7). 6 steps to understanding your potential and achieving more. Lifehack. https://www.lifehack.org/884917/understanding-your-potential
- Hope, T. M. H., Parker Jones, Ō., Grogan, A., Crinion, J., Rae, J., Ruffle, L., Leff, A. P., Seghier, M. L., Price, C. J., & Green, D. W. (2015). Comparing language outcomes in monolingual and bilingual stroke patients. Brain, 138(4), 1070–1083. doi.org/10.1093/brain/awv020
- James, W. (1907). William James: pragmatism: lecture 6: pragmatism's conception of truth. Brocku.ca. https://brocku.ca/MeadProject/James/James_1907/James_1907_06.html
- Jones, A. (2021, March 29). GameStop: What happened, and what it means. International Banker. https://internationalbanker.com/brokerage/gamestop-what-happened-and-what-it-means/
- Kahneman, D. (2011). Thinking, Fast and Slow. Farrar, Straus and Giroux.
- Kahneman, D., & Tversky, A. (1979). Prospect Theory: An Analysis of Decision under Risk. Econometrica, 47(2), 263–292.
- Kenton, W. (2021b, October 5). Sensitivity analysis. Investopedia. https://www.investopedia.com/terms/s/sensitivityanalysis.asp
- King's College London. (2022, February 16). Are attention spans really collapsing? Data shows UK public is worried, but also see technology benefits. Phys.org. https://phys.org/news/2022-02-attention-spans-collapsing-uk-technology.html

- Kostyanaya, M., & Rossouw, P. (2013). Alexander Luria – life, research and contribution to neuroscience. International Journal of Neuropsychotherapy, 1(2), 47–55. doi.org/10.12744/ijnpt.2013.0047-0055
- Lerner, J. S., Li, Y., Valdesolo, P., & Kassam, K. S. (2015). Emotion and Decision Making. Annual Review of Psychology, 66(1), 799–823. doi.org/10.1146/annurev-psych-010213-115043
- Levine, D. S. (2017). Neural network models of human executive function and decision making. ScienceDirect. https://www.sciencedirect.com/topics/psychology/dual-process-theory
- Lim, R. E., & Lee, W. (2022). Communicating corporate social responsibility: How fit, specificity, and cognitive fluency drive consumer
- Skepticism and response. Corporate Social Responsibility and Environmental Management. doi.org/10.1002/csr.2399
- Nassim Nicholas Taleb. (2012). Antifragile : how to live in a world we don't understand. Random House.
- Nassim Nicholas Taleb. (2016). Fooled by randomness : the hidden role of chance in life and in the markets. Random House.
- National Eye Institute. (2019, July 3). Color blindness. Www.nei.nih.gov. https://www.nei.nih.gov/learn-about-eye-health/eye-conditions-and-diseases/color-blindness
- Ogilvy, D. (2013). Confessions of an advertising man. Southbank Publishing.
- Oxford English Dictionary. (n.d.). Critical-thinking noun - Definition, pictures, pronunciation and usage notes. Oxford Learners Dictionaries. Www.oxfordlearnersdictionaries.com. https://www.oxfordlearnersdictionaries.com/definition/english/critical-thinking
- Patterson, K., Grenny, J., Switzler, A., & Mcmillan, R. (2012). Crucial conversations : tools for talking when the stakes are high. Mcgraw-Hill.
- Peterson, L. (2017, November 14). The science behind the art of storytelling. Harvard Business Publishing. https://www.harvardbusiness.org/the-science-behind-the-art-of-storytelling
- Schwartz, B. (2016). The paradox of choice : why more is less. Ecco, An Imprint Of Harpercollins Publishers.
- Shortform. (n.d.). Influence Book summary by Robert B. Cialdini. Shortform. https://www.shortform.com/summary/influence-psychology-of-persuasion-summary-robert-cialdini
- Sloman, S. A. (1996). The empirical case for two systems of reasoning. Psychological Bulletin, 119(1), 3–22. https://doi.org/10.1037/0033-2909.119.1.3

- Song, Z., Roth, R. E., Houtman, L., Prestby, T., Iverson, A., & Gao, S. (2022). Visual Storytelling with Maps. Cartographic Perspectives. https://doi.org/10.14714/cp100.1759
- Stanovich, K. E. (2011). Rationality and the reflective mind. Oxford University Press.
- Takao, S., Clifford, C. W. G., & Watanabe, K. (2019). Ebbinghaus illusion depends more on the retinal than perceived size of surrounding stimuli. Vision Research, 154, 80–84. doi.org/10.1016/j.visres.2018.10.010
- Tardi, C. (2022, July 7). The 80-20 rule (aka Pareto Principle): what it Is, how it Works. Investopedia. https://www.investopedia.com/terms/1/80-20-rule.asp#:~:text=What
- Minto, B. (1987). The Pyramid Principle: Logic in Writing and Thinking. Penguin Books.
- Minto, B. (2010). The Pyramid Principle: Logic in Writing and Thinking. FT Press.
- Stafford, T., & Grimes, A. (2012). Memory Enhances the Mere Exposure Effect. Psychology & Marketing, 29(12), 995–1003. https://doi.org/10.1002/mar.20581
- Winkielman, P., & Cacioppo, J. T. (2001). Mind at ease puts a smile on the face: psychophysiological evidence that processing facilitation elicits positive affect. Journal of Personality and Social Psychology, 81(6), 989–1000. https://pubmed.ncbi.nlm.nih.gov/11761320/
- Winn, H. R. (2017). Dopaminergic System - an overview. ScienceDirect Topics. https://www.sciencedirect.com/topics/psychology/dopaminergic-system
- Asión-Suñer, L., & López-Forniés, I. (2021). Analysis of Modular Design Applicable in Prosumer Scope. Guideline in the Creation of a New Modular Design Model. Applied Sciences. 11(22), 10620. doi.org/10.3390/app112210620

Made in the USA
Las Vegas, NV
31 March 2024

88065113R00134